Mule

Mules as pets

Mule Keeping, Pros and Cons, Care, Costs, Housing, Diet and Health.
by

Roger Rodendale

ALL RIGHTS RESERVED. This book contains material protected under International and Federal Copyright Laws and Treaties.

Any unauthorized reprint or use of this material is strictly prohibited. No part of this book may be reproduced or transmitted in any form or by any means, electronic, mechanical or otherwise, including photocopying or recording, or by any information storage and retrieval system without express written permission from the author.

Copyright © 2017

Published by: IMB Publishing

Table of Contents

Table of Contents 3

Introduction 4

Chapter 1: What is a Mule? 6

Chapter 2: Buying Your Mule.. 18

Chapter 3: Preparing For The Mule..................................... 32

Chapter 4: Bringing The Mule Home................................... 40

Chapter 5: Bonding With Your Mule................................... 52

Chapter 6: Transporting Mules 64

Chapter 7: Mule Health 70

Conclusion... 93

References 94

Introduction

Mules are possibly the most versatile and durable of all farm animals. They are ideal for performing chores on the farm, riding and also packing on a farm. A mule is the offspring of a mare and a male donkey. They have long ears and have a short mane that helps you distinguish between them and the parent animals.

While they are extremely economic to have on a farm, surviving on even low quality feed and forage, they can be quite a handful. The phrase "as stubborn as a mule" has been around all these years for a reason.

According to equine reproduction specialist, Amy McLean, who is associated with the University of California- Davis, you need to make sure that your mule is trained at a really young age. If not they are too stubborn to manage.

On the other hand, when you build a good bond with your mule and learn how to handle them well, you will not only have a good farm animal but also a great companion. When you handle your mule regularly, you will be able to predict his behavior in particular situations and can train him based on how you need to handle him as required.

Once they have been trained, mules retain the knowledge for a long time thanks to their sharp memory. This also applies to the way you treat the animal. For those who are kind and compassionate, the mule will display a lot of trust. But if you cause pain or any form of distress to the animal, he will hold a grudge for a long time.

That is why you need to understand how to work with mules so you can harness their potential as a great pet and farm animal. You also need to give them a good lifestyle that will keep them happy and healthy all through.

This book is designed for those who are contemplating about having a mule as a pet. These animals are wonderful when they are handled well and this book will tell you how you can do that to perfection. Everything that you need to know about mules from choosing a good breed, training them and feeding them, all the details have been discussed in this book in complete detail.

You will also learn about the different ways to build a strong bond with your mule so that you have a pet who will trust you and obey you. Another important subject in this book is the health of your mule. The right feeding practices to make sure that your mule does not get diabetic, protecting them from extreme weather conditions and other factors that have a strong influence on the animal's health are included in this book as well.

Mules require a good amount of time and attention even though they are farm animals that are meant to be outside.

With this book you will learn all about the responsibility of having a mule so that you can decide if you are truly ready to welcome one into your home.

A mule on the left hand side

Chapter 1: What is a Mule?

Mules are a hybrid between a male donkey or jack and a female horse or a mare. These animals are preferred as working animals on farms because they are a lot hardier and also more economical in comparison to horses.

In this chapter, we will learn all about the mule and its specific characteristics that have made it a popular farm animal and also a valuable animal in the military and search and rescue operations. Although they are often associated with traits like stubbornness, mules can make wonderfully obedient pets if trained well.

1. Understanding the mule

The word "mule" is used to describe any hybrid between two different species of the Equine family. This includes a horse, pony and a donkey. Now, in most cases, the word "mule" is associated with a cross between a male donkey and a female horse. It is also used to refer to a cross between a female donkey and a male horse sometimes. But the correct word to describe this hybrid is "hinny".

Basically, the hinny and the mule have one horse parent and one donkey parent. However, they differ quite a bit in stature, appearance and also in their temperament.

2. Differentiating between a horse and a mule

It can be really hard for a novice to tell the difference, as these two animals resemble each other very closely. To begin with, a mule is generally unable to reproduce. Although, there have been instances of female mules being able to produce offspring when mated with a stallion. But, the mule has an odd number of chromosomes. While the horse has 64 and the donkey has 62 chromosomes, the mule has 63, which makes him incapable of reproducing.

The only differentiator between a mule and a horse is the long ears. The mule has much longer ears. Besides that, the muscle quality and composition is quite different. Think about it as comparing the muscles of a ballerina and a football player. Both are gifted with great strength but the performance of the muscle is different.

Similarly, the mule has a lot of physical strength in comparison to its size while the horse is known to have more endurance. While its athletic ability comes from the horse, a mule is known to have acquired its intelligence from the donkey parent.

Surprisingly, donkeys have always been known as slow and stubborn creatures. However, when you interact with them and with mules closely, you will see that the desire for self-preservation and a strong common sense makes these animals very resilient. That is why they seem stubborn.

However, when you are able to treat them with kindness and patience, mules tend to develop a lot of trust. But if you abuse the animal or treat them disrespectfully, they tend to be more inclined to resisting. Horses, on the other hand are not as stubborn or resistant as a mule when being domesticated.

3.Difference between donkey and mule

The biggest difference between the donkey and the mule is the origin. Donkeys are descendants of a species of African Wild Ass. They belong to the same family as the horse but are an entirely different species. It is believed that donkeys were bred about 5000 years ago in Egypt and Mesopotamia.

Mules as we know, are a hybrid between a mare and a male donkey or jack. This is why genetics is believed to be the biggest differentiator between a donkey and a mule. While the mule has 63 chromosomes, an odd number, donkeys have 62.

Besides that there are also physical traits that make it easy to differentiate between a mule and a horse. The coat of the mule resembles a horse more closely and is not coarse like the hair on a donkey. During the winter months, however, the coat of the mule begins to resemble a donkey.

One more feature is the fifth lumbar which is present in a mule and a horse and not in a donkey.

The sound made by the animals also helps you distinguish between them besides these physical traits. The bray of a donkey is a very clear hee-haw. On the other hand, the sound made by the mule sounds like a mix of the whinny of a horse and the bray of a donkey. It begins as a whinny and then moves into a hee-haw.

4.Mule distinct traits

So to summarize, here are the common traits of the mule that will help you identify one:

- The bray is unique to the species.
- The animal resembles the horse more than a donkey.
- Hair is present only at the end of the tail unlike horses.
- The mane is thin, upright and short.

- There are several color varieties that are available.
- The ears are extremely long.
- The hoof is box like and is very narrow unlike that of the horse. This is what makes them able to stand for long hours and navigate through a variety of different terrains such as mountains and rocky areas. The hoof is elastic and very tough. It does not chip very easily and when left untrimmed can grow quite a bit. It also tends to grow faster when the animal is raised on a soft ground.
- The body is long and has wiry muscles.
- The back is straight and short. The withers are not distinct making the mule the perfect animal to bear a lot of weight.
- The bone is hard and very dense.
- Gestation period of mules lasts for about 12 months while that of a horse is usually 11 months.
- The belly and the muzzle are covered with white fur. You will also have a circle of white fur around the eyes of the animal.
- Their body conformation lies in between a horse and a donkey.
- Usually, the best traits of the dam and the sire are passed on to a mule. For instance, the physical strength is derived from the horse while the intelligence and the hardiness comes from the donkey.

Indeed, mules are excellent companions when trained properly and raised under conditions that promote health and well-being.

5. History of the mule

Although the exact history of the mule's origin is unknown, it is safe to say that they have been a part of human civilization from the very beginning. As proof of that, the animal has been mentioned in the Book of Genesis when it was first laid out in parchment.

In fact, the mules were considered a lot more valuable than chariot horses among the Hittites. Even the biblical kings of Israel favored the mule as a better choice of transport.

While it is impossible to say when the first ever mule was bred, there is enough evidence to suggest that these animals were deliberately included as part of domesticated animals even in ancient times. While the most common method of creating hybrids is to mate a mare with a male donkey, there is also evidence that a stud or male horse and a female donkey were interbred to create the hybrid.

It is believed that the inhabitants of Nicaie and Paphlagonia, which is now part of northern Turkey, were the first ones to have bred mules. These animals were common in Egypt even before the time of Moses.

According to the Greek writer and historian, Homer, mules were brought in from Henetia, located in Asia Minor where breeding them was a specialty. This record was made as early as 800BC in the Iliad.

This is when the donkey was replaced by the mule as the royal beast. It was rode by King Solomon and King David when they were being coroneted.

The mule was introduced to the new world by Christopher Colombus, who bought two Jennies and four Jack donkeys along with his horses. While exploring the Americas, the Conquistadors from Mexico also used mules.

George Washington is known across the globe as the father of America. What is interesting is that he was also the first breeder of Mules in America. He was known for his skills as a horseman. There are legends of him covering 120 miles on horseback in just two days. Washington also had an avid interest in agriculture. This is why he understood the importance of the mule as a farm animal. He recognized the beasts for being hardier, more economic and more long-lived than horses. This is when he began to breed them.

Towards the mid-1700s, Spain became popular for its high quality jackasses. The animals that were bred in this region were known for being remarkably strong. They also had more endurance than other specimens bred globally. The Monarch wanted to preserve these traits in his homeland and hence, banned the export of these mules.

It was only in 1784 that King Charles III, the then ruler of Spain, agreed to send three Jennies and two Spanish Jacks to Mount Vernon for George Washington. While one of the jacks did not survive the journey, the one that did was given to Washington in December 1785. This jack was named Royal Gift to honor the ruler of Spain.

Unfortunately, Royal Gift did not mate with any of the 30 mares that were prepared for him. It was clear that the exhausting journey took a toll on him. It was only in spring the following year that Royal Gift was mated to give rise to the mule breeding business in America.

A census conducted in Mount Vernon in the year 1799 showed 130 horses but no traces of mules. In the same year, after Washington died, 58 mules and 25 horses were listed in the census. In less than two decades, there were close to 855,000 working mules in the USA alone!

In Kentucky, by the year 1840, it was possible to earn about $5000 with a high quality jack that was solely used to breed mules. The number of mules in America rose to 22 million by 1897 when the cotton boom occurred. The farmer bulletin no.1311 that was issued by the US Department of Agriculture was titled "Mule Production". This publication provided all the necessary details to breed a good stock of mules successfully. It also listed all the traits of mules.

Between the years 1829 and 1849, a pack of mules were trained to carry about 200 pounds of supplies on the Spanish Trail connecting Los Angeles and Santa Fe. This trail that was about 2700 miles long was believed to be the most difficult one to navigate. The mules were faster than horses on this track and were also better at carrying the supplies. While horses and oxen could pull wagon trails up to five miles a day, mules were able to cover 30 miles. Stage coaches in the West also used mules instead of horses because they were able to travel on the flat dry land at an average of 5 miles per hour. They could travel for hours while horses would give up long before this.

The US Army had several mule units of which the last two were deactivated at fort Carson, Colo in 1957. Recently, mules have been reintroduced in these combat units at the US Marine Corps Mountain Warfare Training Centre in California. These units are specifically being trained to navigate through Afghanistan and other high altitude areas.

A decline in mule population in the USA was noted in the year 1960. This was prevented due to the collective efforts of several breeders who wanted to keep the species thriving in the United States. Betsy Hutchins and Paul Hutchins founded the American Donkey and Mule Society in the year 1967.

The sole purpose of this society was to make sure that the long years were protected and understood better. To do this, a bi-monthly magazine named Brayer was also introduced. Today there are several trade publications, stock shows and TV programs like the Meredith Series that educate people about these wonderful animals.

The mule has, no doubt, played a significant part in human civilization. In fact, it has contributed to advancements of several fields, including agriculture, and is considered one of the most important of all domesticated animals.

6.Understanding infertility in mules
While mules are the best of both worlds for those looking for a strong and resilient farm animal, the fact that they are sterile makes it hard to breed

more of them unless you are able to find a horse and a donkey that you can mate.

Many farm owners wait for their female mules or mollies to foal but it is very unlikely as there have been very few reported cases of mules giving birth.

We have read that the mules have only 63 chromosomes while the donkey has 62 and the horse has 64. The question is why one chromosome affects an entire species. And, the answer lies in careful understanding of cell division that is the basis of reproduction.

There are two types of cell division- mitosis and meiosis. Now, we know that cells contain DNA, which is the genetic construction of every living being. The DNA in our body is organized in the form of chromosomes. The difference in the number of chromosomes determines the traits of different species. For instance, humans have 46 chromosomes while the earthworm has 36 and a goldfish has about 100. These numbers are even because the chromosomes are paired to form homologous pairs. Homologous means that the genes in these two chromosomes are organized in the same order. For example, with humans, there are 23 pairs of chromosomes. It is the 15th pair that contains the gene for brown eyes on both chromosomes.

When the cell contains a nucleus, a process called mitosis occurs to create new cells when the parent cell divides. When the cells divide through this process, a duplicate of the chromosome is formed and the cell splits into two parts after the membrane of the nucleus dissolves. Now you have two cells that contain the exact same chromosomes.

This process is the basis of all life whether it is a human being or a goldfish cell. There are trillions of cells that divide to create one being.

That brings us to the mules and the reason for their sterility. For sexual reproduction to occur, the offspring receives half the amount of necessary chromosomes from one parent and the other half from the other parent. This means that you get one chromosome from each homologous pair.

Once the chromosomes are duplicated, the original homologous pair and the duplicated ones will align. That is why some traits are crossed over. This means that you can have your grandma's eyes and your grandpa's height, for instance.

After the crossover occurs, these homologous pairs separate from one another and the cell divides. What you have as a result of this is that there are four cells that will have one chromosome each from the first homologous pair.

In the case of mules, the odd number results in one chromosome not having a homologous pair. As a result, the process of cell division breaks down leading to infertility. This is one of the most common occurrences in species created by interbreeding two different species. Very rarely will the female be sterile.

This is why breeding mules means that you will have to look for a horse and a donkey whose traits you want in the resulting offspring. Breeding by mating mules gives you very slim, almost negligible chances of success.

7. Personality of the mule

While the fact that they are hardy and very efficient makes these animals popular on farms, they are also preferred choices for pets in many households. This is solely because of the wonderful demeanor and the interesting personality of mules. While they are usually only associated with the adjective "stubborn", there is a lot more to the mule when you actually decide to make one your companion.

The attitude of the mule makes him a rather unique animal. Even when you are buying your first mule, you will notice that the attitude of the mule is the first thing that will strike you, long before the physical conformation of the animal.

A lot of breeders vouch for the fact that you can understand the demeanor of a mule just by looking into his eyes. With most of them, you will see the "kind eye" which shows that the animal is kind, playful, docile and extremely trusting of people in general.

Very rarely do people notice fear or any aggressive traits in the eyes of a mule. These mules do exist and should never be your choice for a pet, if you are a first timer. It is very hard to change the attitude of the mule. These attitude issues most often tend to develop from injuries or mishandling by people. Remember, the mule has a strong sense of self preservation and will not tolerate any abusive behavior.

Mules have often, quite wrongly, been labelled as stubborn. The fact is that these animals look out for themselves because of that sense of self preservation. That is why, when a mule sees a problem, he will try to find the best way to get out of that problem. If he feels like his way is better than the way you are showing him, he is not one to follow blindly.

This is one of the main reasons why persuading a mule can seem like an uphill task to most people, while it actually can be done with immense patience.

Another reason why a mule can come across as stubborn and not as a natural follower is because these creatures are highly intelligent. Extensive research has been carried out to demonstrate the cognitive abilities of mules. The results have left many stunned as mules tend to have better problem solving skills than donkeys and horses.

These animals are also quicker to respond to different situations or stimuli. They are known to be good learners. They can learn good habits just as easily as they can learn the bad ones. As a result, for first time owners it is very important to know the behavior and the psychology of mules before bringing them home. When you are training them, you should be able to get it right the first time.

The most important trait of a mule is that he is an independent thinker. That is why, when you are training a mule you need to make sure that he is a willing partner in the process. You should be able to show the mule that what you expect of him is reasonable and advantageous to him.

Mules are known to have a lot of common sense. This is what makes them great trail animals. They are not ones who will panic or be careless in a situation that may even startle them. They will analyze a situation thoroughly and then react.

Mules are extremely alert which makes them great guard animals. They are uncannily sensitive to danger. When these animals are used in difficult terrain, you can trust them completely. If a mule refuses to set foot in a certain area, you can be sure that the land is loose or some danger prevails. The best part is that you will be completely safe as you can never persuade a mule to walk where there is any inkling of danger.

Mules require company. For instance, if you have a stable with several mules, they will like to be close to their friends. This could be another mule, a donkey, a horse or even a cow or goat. If they are taken away from their companions for a few days or weeks, he will not perform as well as he used to before.

In this time of separation, mules look for another companion, preferably the same species that they had initially formed a bond with. If they cannot find this, they will settle for any other companion such as a dog.

That said, it is possible to make your mule independent. This can be done by separating him from his buddy for some time every day. You can also change the field mates on a regular basis. Independence is one of the most desirable qualities in mules. This can be retained with proper training measures.

Of course, they develop strong bonds with people although they take their time to build that trust. These animals will seem suspicious at first and may even seem frightened or aloof. This can be changed with frequent interaction, especially with the younger ones. These animals are also curious by nature, which makes them responsive to your attempts to befriend him.

Once a mule allows you to handle him, he will trust you completely and will actually make a wonderful companion.

A mule is known for being extremely docile. As a result they have also been used regularly as therapy animals. When trained completely, these animals can be used for therapeutic riding programs that are especially popular with children.

With children who have any developmental issues, mules can lead to tremendous mental and physical improvement with constant interaction. They are also great to induce positive interactions between families and members of the community.

There are special riding programs that have been extended to children with autism, at-risk children, wounded veterans and soldiers and other special requirement groups through camps and regular riding programs.

Mules, especially the miniature ones, are preferred because they are gentler and are also small enough for children to ride them easily. The transformations that mules have brought about in the lives of people is truly commendable.

If you are able to provide a mule with the necessary space and a life that promotes well-being and solid training, you will have a great companion for life. The more you learn about them, the easier it will be to create this special bond.

8.Interesting mule facts

Mules are not as dull as they are played out to be. These animals are quite extraordinary in several ways that will make you wonder why you did not bring home a mule sooner.

- They are among the most maintenance free equines. In comparison to horses, these animals tend to have fewer hoof and leg problems. They have fewer medical issues overall. They can work on soft ground even without being shod. It is only when they work on stony or concrete ground that you will need to shoe them.

- They have a very tough and robust skin.

- They have a much longer life span than other equines. While a horse lives up to 30 years, a mule can live for close to 50 years. Usually horses are productive only up to the age of 15-18 years. Mules on the other hand, can be used on farms for close to 30-40 years for activities like riding.

- The quantity of food required by these animals is a lot lesser than other agricultural animals. They also have a very efficient digestive system, which means that they will only require food equal to 1.5% of their body weight. Of course, this varies depending upon the type of work that they do on the farm. But when a horse and a mule are given the same amount of work, the mule will require less food.

- They are much stronger in comparison to other equines. They are more agile and have more stamina. They are superior to donkeys in terms of size as they are usually a lot larger than donkeys, being about to carry more load than them.

- These animals make great guards for livestock. This is a function that they share with the donkey. However, a mule is not as aggressive as a donkey. They are also not like horses who prefer flight to fight.

- Their sense of self-preservation is extremely strong which is why they are good guard animals. They are most likely to be a better companion in case of an attack by a wild animal or a predator. These animals are also a lot better on farms where they will never allow themselves to be overworked to the point of death, unlike horses.

- If you are riding a mule in a storm or in areas like the Grand Canyon, they are a lot more surefooted than equines like horses. They are also not as easily spooked which makes them more trustworthy.

- They are very hardy animals. Since they have the genes of the donkey who originated from arid lands, they can tackle heat and a lack of water very well.

- The first time a mule, who is usually sterile, was cloned successfully was at the University of Idaho in the year 2003, in conjunction with the State University of Utah.

- Mules come in a variety of colors including brown, black, copper red, bay or reddish brown, dun, roans, buckskin, palomino and white.

- A mule has the ability to carry 20% of his own body weight on his back. However, if a person is riding him, he can carry close to 30% of his own body weight.

- Mules are sometimes produced specifically for a sport called mule-jumping which is a type of race. For these mules, a thoroughbred mare is used. When mules are produced to be able to walk over long trails, they are bred from a quarter horse.

- Mules have the ability to kick with their hooves in every direction, even sideways!

- Draft mules are the larger varieties of mules that are produced by breeding draft horses such as mammoth jacks or even Belgian horses that are large in size as well.

- There are some mules that are trained to specifically be commercial pack mules. These mules work in areas with tough terrains and rugged roads and are used to mostly transport goods. There are 16 commercial mule pack stations in the United States in the Sierra Nevada region.

- Mules are also used for entertainment. They are part of several competitions such as show jumping, dressage and English pleasure riding. As a result, their popularity among hobby breeders has also been constantly on the rise.

- In the Sierra Nevada region, the US Army has a special Mountain Warfare Training Center where the mules and the riders are trained for 11 days at a stretch.

- China is considered to be the world's largest market for producing and using mules. They are followed by Mexico.

There is no doubt that these animals have become an important part of the human civilization serving not only as farm animals but also in warfare and transportation. Besides that, mules make great pets because of their docile nature and their ability to adapt to new families quite easily.

In most urban settings, space is quite the constraint when you are considering having a mule as a pet. To resolve this dilemma, miniature mules have been bred by several mule enthusiasts. These animals measure less than 50" at the withers and can make wonderful pets.

Chapter 2: Buying Your Mule

The best place to buy your mule from is from a reputed breeder. There are also several cattle and livestock expos where mules are generally sold. When you decide to buy a mule, you need to make sure that you bring home a healthy one.

1. Consider a few things

Before you decide to bring a mule home, you need to make sure that you know why you are buying one. There are several things that a mule can do on your farm besides being wonderful pets. Some common mule functions include:

- Trail rides
- Driving
- Packing
- Shows

Once you know why exactly you want your mule, you can narrow down your options and look for the prefect mule. It is best that you consider the following points before you actually begin to look for the ideal mule for your home:
- What is your budget for the mule? It is best that you buy a mule that does not require you to overspend. It is possible that you will find a mule and fall in love with it completely. That should not be an excuse to buy one that is beyond a budget. It is a better idea to look hard for an animal that can fit into all your requirements and your budget.

- How much experience do you have with equines? If you have never ridden or even owned a horse, then dealing with a mule is a bigger challenge. These animals are very sharp and are quick to take advantage of you if you make any mistakes when you are training them. You need to be able to understand the psychology of equines and understand the body language of these animals before you commit to one.

- Do you have the patience for a mule? With mules it is not so much about physical strength as it is your wits. You can never force the animal to do anything. What you should be able to do is convince them that they ought to do it. That will require a lot of patience and perseverance from your end.

- Are you in for the mind games? Mules are thinking animals with great cognitive skills. They are very different from horses and will always look for a good mental challenge before they accept your command or just stay interested in what you are trying to communicate with them. You need to be very careful when you train them. If they get bored, you must stop. If they respond well, shower them with praises. If the mule gets angry or annoyed, just forget about training him for that day.

- Do you have the facilities your mule needs? There are several things that you will have to take care of such as shelter and fencing. The best option would be an electric fence as mules find their way around any other type of fence.

- Will your mule have any companions? Mules are very friendly animals and will only do well with companionship. They do not need their own kind or humans for that. They will get attached to just about any animal on your farm. They become herd bound with horses, especially when mares are around. This can become a hassle when the mule needs to be separated from the herd. Mules can find friends in sheep, goats or dogs. But the problem of trampling them always remains. There are several instances of smaller animals being trampled accidentally or when the mule gets into a bad mood. As for children, never leave them with the mule unattended unless the child is old enough to understand how to approach a mule correctly.

- Do you have any riding experience? You will have to find a mule based on the type of riding that you are comfortable with. If you are looking for a mule, he should conform to the physical and mental attributes that are suited for you. When buying a young mule, you can get a lot of hints from the parents. While the conformation and the physical attributes are inherited from the Jack, a mule is mostly very similar to the mother when it comes to attitude and disposition. This will help you understand what to expect from your mule.

2.Where to look

There are several options available to source a mule from. While the most common one remains a reputed breeder, you can consider the following options as well:

Auction Arenas

You will find special auction arenas that take place usually in the warmer months. They can also be part of country fairs that showcase several types of livestock for sale. Now, an auction arena is a great place to look at several mules at one time.

However, it is never recommended that novices buy mules from these auction arenas. This is because you do not get enough time to examine the mule or have him checked by a vet for any existing health conditions. If you want to shop at an auction, you must take a breeder or a mule dealer to go with you to find the perfect mule for you.

Online Bidding

This is one of the latest high tech innovations in the world of livestock buying. Live auctions are online biddings that will allow you to choose from several mules at once. A buyer can bid on a mule from his home after getting linked to any company that has set up special cameras for the mules on sale or is specialized in broadcasting on the Internet.

The advantage of online bidding is that distance is never a barrier. You can find the perfect mule for yourself even if you are across the country. You will require a good Internet service that provides good speed in order to be able to make the bid in time. You can also save a lot of time and money that you would have otherwise spent travelling to these livestock auctions. If you are a first time buyer, it will help to have an experienced mule owner or breeder help you pick.

Mule dealers

There are several reputed mule breeders who either have mules of their own or are in collaboration with breeders. They will be able to find the perfect mule for your home. The advantage of looking for a mule with a dealer is that you will be able to get a firsthand experience of the mule's behavior. You can observe the dealer or the owner catch, harness or hitch the mule to a cart. Then, you can try it yourself to see if the disposition of the mule is suitable for you.

Once you have chosen a mule, the dealer will have him transported to your home. You can even keep them on a probation period that will allow you to test out how comfortable you are with managing the mule. You can send in a check only when you are entirely sure that you can keep the mule with you.

You can look for mule dealers on the Internet. Make sure that you read up reviews or ask for recommendations from others who own mules before you make a commitment and actually buy your mule.

Mule breeders

You will be able to find both professional breeders and hobby breeders who will be able to show you a choice of mules of different colors and ages. These breeders choose the best mares and jacks to produce healthy mules that can be used for different functions on your farm. You can look for breeders who specialize in certain mules. Some of them breed mules especially for showing while others will be able to give you the ideal mule for packing and riding. This will depend entirely on the purpose that you are buying your mules for. You will also be able to find miniature mules with breeders.

The biggest disadvantage with buying from breeders is that they usually deal with very young mules. These mules require training and unless you have any help to do so or have the experience to do it yourself, it is never a good idea to buy a young mule. It is best that you look for breeders who deal with "broke" mules. These mules have been trained to follow basic cues and are able to perform tasks like following you on a lead or allowing you to ride them or use them for packing.

Classified Ads

There are several advertisements for the private sale of mules. This is the best place for first time buyers to look for a mule. There are advertisements online or in newspapers that you should keep your eye on when you decide to bring a mule home.

Even with these ads, it is best that you take along a mentor who can help you find a mule to suit your requirements. You must always shop around a little before you buy a mule. If after looking at multiple options, you find that one of the earlier ones that you saw is suitable for you, you can always go back.

When you buy from private ads, you must do some research on what the right price for a mule is. While there are several factors such as the age, the coat color and the build that determine the cost, you must always stay clear of any scams. For this you can go through newsletters by popular breeders or even speak to mule owners to understand what you can expect to pay for a certain mule. If you can take someone with more experience along, make sure that you interact with the mule before you buy it.

Rescue shelters

Another great option is to adopt a mule from a shelter. Mules are not the easiest animals to care for if you do not have the experience and the patience for it. This is why several mules are abandoned each year and are left in shelters.

These mules could be in perfect condition health-wise but may require some work to alter unfavorable behavior that they may have acquired because of mistakes made by the previous owners. This is why first time owners should acquire as much information possible and gain some experience with mules before they decide to adopt one.

Most shelters have functioning and updated websites that you can look for a mule on. They will have all the pictures of the animals on display for you to choose from. Once you have finalized which one you want to adopt, you will be required to visit the shelter and interact with him to understand if he is suitable for you or not.

In most cases, adoption is free of cost. However, some may charge an adoption fee to cover for any medical expenses borne by the shelter towards the mule. There are a few shelters that insist that you attend classes in house and spend a minimum number of hours interacting with the mule that you have chosen to gain some experience.

Following this, you will have to fill out an adoption form and submit it with the necessary details. When you have finished all the processes involved with adoption, you will have to be available for a house check. Once the volunteers approve of your residence and facilities, you can take the mule home. Most often shelters will not arrange for transport. However, some of them will be willing to meet you at a convenient place to pick your mule up from.

No matter what source you choose for your mule, the important thing to remember is that you need to choose the right mule for you. The physical and mental attributes should be suitable for you to handle the mule comfortably. The next section gives you all the details about choosing the perfect mule.

If you are a first timer, it is advisable that you spend some time handling the mule at the breeder or the dealer's farm before you bring him home. That way you will be able to train yourself to handle him well.

3. Choosing the mule

There are some things that you need to keep in mind when you are buying the mule. You need to make sure that the mule is healthy and of good disposition so he can fit into your family perfectly.

In this section you will find all the details that you need to find a perfect mule.

Check the conformation

We have discussed the general physical traits of the mule in the first chapter. The conformation of a mule refers to the visual appeal of the animal. For this, it is a good idea to educate yourself about the different horse breeds that exist so you can have a fair idea about what you need to look for.

For most people, the more closely a mule fits into the physical standards of a horse, the more appealing he is. When you are choosing the mule, picture the different varieties of horses that you are familiar with. There are the refined and high strung thoroughbreds who have a stronger bone structure. Then you have quarter horses that are stockier but a more sensible choice. These horses come with a coarse bone structure and are known to be as docile as the Belgian draft horses.

The reason you should compare them to horses is that these mules are the offspring of a variety of horse breeds and usually inherit their looks from the horse parent. You will be able to find mules of various sizes and shapes, with different temperaments. Even if two mules look completely different from one another, they can have the perfect conformation depending upon the horse parent. When you notice visual differences in mules, understand that these are merely the breed type rather than any faults in the conformation.

Even if you are a novice or an amateur, you will be able to tell if the mule has a good conformation. Just analyze how the body parts flow into one another. If you notice any questionable development of the mule, then you are probably noticing a conformation issue.

The rule of thumb is that the body should be visually pleasant. The muscles should look smooth and the body must look well balanced. You must take a look at as many mules as possible in order to get a better eye to look into the overall conformation of a mule before you buy one.

You will also get a lot of clues from the gait of the mule. Watch them walk, run or carry a load on their back. If they seem sluggish or seem to be unable to take strong and even strides when they are walking, then there are chances that they have some developmental issues.

The coat should also be smooth and should not have any bald patches or matting. These are signs of poor management. With poorly managed mules, you will also have the chances of several behavioral issues that are the result of it.

It is also a good idea to know exactly what you are looking for in a mule before you choose one. That way, you will be able to pick one that closely resembles the picture that you have in your mind for the ideal mule for your household or your farm.

Disposition

The disposition or the attitude of the mule is everything when you are choosing one. You will be able to understand the general traits or characteristics of the mule when you watch him interact with the owner. You can decide about the disposition of the mule based on how he rides, packs and drives.

The saddle mule

The most common type of mule that people look for is a saddle mule. The first thing to do is to ask the owner to bring the mule out of the saddle. If he is saddled already, then it could be a red flag. There are several things that you will not be able to learn with a mule that has already been saddled.

For instance, the mule could be really hard to catch, he may not take to the saddle willingly or may have other bad behaviors that you will not be able to notice. It is ideal that the mule greets the owner at the gate when he approaches to saddle him. If the mule turns away or goes away in the other direction, it is the sign of some possible issue.

The next thing you will observe is the reaction of the mule to the halter. They should ideally put their nose into the halter willingly. Then, the mule's ease of being led should be taken into account. As the owner leads the mule, you should see that there is enough slack in the rope which shows that he is willing to be led. If not, you will see that the owner has to drag the lead.

Mules are brushed before they are saddled. The ideal thing for the mule is to stand and enjoy the brushing and pay heed to what the person brushing him is saying. Mules actually enjoy conversations when they are being brushed. Mules should ideally be familiar with a few words that are part of their vocabulary including get over and whoa. Of these words whoa is the most important one as it means come to a complete standstill.

The owner will then tap each hoof with a hammer. At this point, he should not pull away or lean on the owner. The ears and tail are great indicators of the mule's comfort level. The tail must stand quietly and should not be held up. The ears should not be stiff, rather relaxed.

Once this is all done, the mule is ready to be saddled. This is when you need to watch the bridle. If the ears fit in easily and move into place, then it is a good sign. However, if there is a need to unbuckle the bridle, the mule could have ear-shying issues. This can take a lot of time to fix and can be the beginning of several other behavioral issues.

The mule's response to the reign will tell you a lot. Ideally, after the reign is in place, the mule should stand still waiting for the rider to give him a command. This could include walking forward, backward or taking one step at a time etc. This is a sign of good training.

Should you see the mule with a saddle on already, have the owner take it off and then examine the back. You should not be able to see any white spots on the back. This is an indication that the saddle has not been fitted properly. Normally, mules will bob their heads up and down as an indication that the saddle is not in place or is uncomfortable. If you do not pay attention, they will get to a point when they begin to show other severe symptoms like kicking the saddle or jumping around unexpectedly. The bigger the white spots, the longer the mule has been saddled improperly.

If you notice any scars on the back, make sure you enquire about them. You can ask for details such as where the mule comes from or about any untoward incidents that may have occurred when riding or leading him.

The next thing you will do is to ask the owner to saddle the mule. The mule must not become goosey or irritable when this is done. After the saddling is done, ask the seller to mount the mule. The mule must stand still until a command is given.

You must ask the owner to back the mule up first and then move ahead. This will give you a chance to observe the response to leg cues. The rider should not have to pull on the reign too hard to get the mule to respond. The lighter the mule is on the bit, the better trained he is.

Once you have made all these observations, take some time to think. If you feel like this is the mule you would like to buy, you must try to spend some time with him before you bring him home. You can set up appointments to lead the mule or even ride him to understand how well he can be handled by people other than the owner. Just walk around with the mule a few times to get a fair idea about his attitude and level of training that he has been given.

How does the mule drive?

The attitude or the disposition of the mule when being driven is just as important as his behavior when he is being saddled. You must learn all that you need to about the foundation training for driving given to the mule.

Make sure that he is driven without blinders. It is true that mules are a lot happier when they are able to look at what is going on around them. Then, you can ask questions such as the beginning of driving training. Ask if it started with tires and poles? How long did it take before he was actually driven? A foundation training program that is about a month long is ideal. Did the mule learn alone or with other mules and does he drive single and double? These questions will give you an idea about the foundation training of the mule.

Then you will see how easy he is to handle. The mule should be easy to catch. Ideally, a mule will approach you voluntarily when you walk up to the corral. When he is being haltered, he should tip his nose towards you and drop his head.

You know that the mule should be comfortable when he is being led. The next thing is to check his response to being hooked to a wagon. Before that, you can watch how the mule drives when he is hooked to a tire or a pole.

Irrespective of what he is being hooked to, whether it is a wagon or a tire, the mule must walk over to the object and stand quietly as the owner hooks him. Then you can ask for the mule to be hooked to a wagon. After this has been done, the mule must not start moving ahead on his own.

He should wait for commands whether it is to move forward, back, to the left or to the right. When he starts moving, the head should be straight and should not tip to one side.

When you are taking the mule to the street, watch how he reacts to the gate being opened. Is he waiting calmly or is he impatient to just get out the door? Any impatience is a learnt trait and is not really the fault of the mule.

The mule should not require a slap with a line on the back to move. A mule who is well trained will begin to move when he is asked to.

The real test is when the mule is taken out on the road. There are several distractions such as vehicles or people walking around. There could also be humps on the road that can make pulling a wagon difficult.

The mule should not be affected by sounds and different sights. Instead, the ears should be relaxed and the trail should be swaying gently as he leads the wagon. If you notice that his ears are straight up, then he is probably not comfortable. The tail should not switch too often but must just hang and move with each stride naturally.

Observing a mule when he drives can give you a lot of detail about the training that the mule has been given. To understand how to test the driving skills of the mule, it is a good idea to educate yourself by talking to other mule owners or by reading books and visiting clinics who normally treat mules at their facility.

How does the mule pack?

The way a mule responds to your authority will tell you a lot about the mule. The mule must be willing to befriend you. In addition to that, he should be willing to go where you want him to go and should be willing to follow your command. The mule should have quiet eyes and must not snort or show any anxiety when you approach him. That shows a willing nature.

For mules that are designed to pack, a medium bone conformation is preferred. The head should be inclined straight up out of his shoulder. The longer the ears of the mule, the better. Good withers with round hips are a big bonus for mules that are intended to be packing animals. You will buy a mule that is suitable for your own height. Mules are usually measured in "hands". That means that for someone who is shorter, a mule that is about 14 hands in size is ideal.

For a mule to become a good pack mule, it is necessary for you to provide him with a lot of training. Lots of people think otherwise and believe that packing mules do not need any training. Packing also requires a certain level of knowledge and some foundation training for the mule before you can make him a saddle mule.

There are several training aids that you can use. You can use hot walkers, hitching posts, front leg hobbles and also tie the mule to a trailer. With these techniques, the mule learns to be patient. It is not enough for a mule to just stand in a corral. Then, whenever you take them outside, they tend to paw, jump and even move around quite a bit. This can make it hard for you to pack a mule. Keeping them tied out will help them understand that they need to stay where you want them to. That way, they will be of pleasant disposition even outside the corral.

There are several books on packing mules that you can refer to. One common piece of information in all these books is to pack the mules in such a way that they do not get scared. In some cases, owners like to add several tin boxes or rattles in while packing the mule, on purpose. That way the mule will sack out and will not be startled or scared with any noise.

Preparing for riding and final sacking is necessary before you go on actual trails. Sometimes, mules tend to bump into obstacles on the way when they are not properly trained. In case of an experienced pack, they will be able to step aside and continue on the trail without the pack boxes hitting any obstacles that may be in the way.

A good trait of a pack mule is that he should stand still when he is being packed. Normally, pack boxes and bags are orange in color. This is not an issue as mules are color blind and will not be startled with these colors normally. Using the right packing material will help the mule get adjusted to the sound and also the weight.

He will also need to practice opening a tarp and pulling it over the packing boxes. If he is not used to this, there are chances that he will be quite startled at the end of it. Watch how the mule takes each step. A packing mule should be willing to give his leg to the owner. This is necessary to teach him to accept a tarp. This will also help you shoe the mule and take care of his foot when he is required to pack.

When you are observing the packing behavior of the mule, you will have to check how he reacts to the lash rope. If the rope slaps the mule on the belly, the mule tends to react in an unpleasant manner. These ropes are usually 30-40 feet long and you need to have a mule of great disposition to let you go around completely.

If the owner is able to get the lash rope around, then it means that he trusts humans completely. You see, getting the lash rope around requires the owner to take the rope under the belly, around the legs and over the back. Unless the mule trusts completely, he will never let anyone do this.

Another interesting thing to watch is how the mule responds to being on trail with other mules. If he is able to get along, then he is probably very patient and calm in general.

When you get to interact with a pack mule for the first time, it can be extremely exciting. You will get to observe how the mule is halter trained, how good his foundation training is and how comfortably he allows someone to lead him.

If the mule halter is using a chain that goes under the chin and over the nose, it means that the mule is not properly halter trained. One who is easy with the halter will only need a rope halter.

For a pack mule, physical condition is of great importance. You are essentially packing in dead weight on his back. That means he needs to have enough endurance to bear the weight. If you are looking for a good pack mule, he should be given good foundation training. It is not possible to just take the mule out one day and put the outfit on his back.

If the mule has not been conditioned by the owner, you have to be sure that you will be able to train the mule for this. There are various tools and techniques but what is more important is that you need to have the patience to be able to teach the mule how to wear a packing outfit.

In general, when you are looking for mules to drive, pack or ride, here are a few traits that you need to look for:

- Good disposition
- Good physical condition
- Ability to stand in place when being mounted or groomed
- Easy to catch
- Easy to lead
- Gets along with other equines
- Medium to heavy bone structure
- Good trailing
- Easy to shoe
- Good conformation

While it is good to observe the mule being led, driven and packed, you should also give it a shot on your own before you decide upon the mule that you want to bring home. It is especially necessary to ride the mule alone if that is what you want to buy one for. As for leading, you can walk the mule around and see how easily he follows you.

4. Points to consider when you buy

There are a few points that you will have to keep in mind before you make your final purchase:

- In case the mule has been shown he should have a record of the accomplishments. If the owner just tells you he "has been shown", you will have to check what classes he has been shown in. For instance, one who has been shown in a halter class will not necessarily know how to perform under saddle or in a harness. You should ask about the classes that the mule has been entered in, how he performed, who handled him, how many shows he entered and when.

- The mule must sell itself. You should be convinced of the personality, behavior and performance of the mule before you buy him. You will rarely find a seller who can guarantee good disposition. In many cases, mules are usually abandoned because of bad habits and behavior that result from injuries or bad handling.

- Do not hesitate to ask questions about the mule. Make sure you ask about the history of the mule, any personality quirks, behaviors, habits and the history of the mule's training. You should be confident that you can handle the animal. In case the mule has been trained by a professional, you must ask about the trainer. It is never good for a mule to be trained by someone who generally trains horses. If the seller does not know everything about the mule, you should look for some answers yourself. A veterinary check, for instance, is a good way to learn about issues related to the hoof or the general health of the mule.

- You must ask the seller why the mule is on sale. If you feel like the reasons do not sound genuine, it is a good idea to rely on your instincts. If you have any doubt, double check. It is always good to be cautious about mules. You should be able to assess the thoughts, concerns, experience and priority of the seller before you commit.

- If you do not know anything about buying mules, always take someone with sound knowledge with you. That way, you will be able to notice several points that you may have missed otherwise. It is advised even for knowledgeable equine buyers to take someone along.

- The seller must always be asked to demonstrate. You may want to see the mule being caught in an open area. In most cases, the older the animal, the harder he is to catch. Then, you can ask for a riding demonstration that will help you decide if you have enough experience to handle him. The animal should have experience with all the work that you intend for him to do on your farm.

- When you have a farm with other animals, make sure you ask about how the mule behaves with certain animals. For instance, some mules may not be comfortable with calves or colts but may get along with cows and horses.

- Having a vet check every mule that you review can be expensive. It is a good idea to learn about the general health issues that you need to check. For instance, you should be able to assess hoof health and other basics. There are several books that will give you tips. You can also consult an equine vet to show you how to do this.

- Once you find a mule that you think is good enough for your farm or home, then have him thoroughly checked by the vet for general health and soundness. This is a step that you must never neglect.

- It is a good idea to test the animal out in an environment that is similar to yours. You must ride and lead the mule as much as you can. The environment is very important. For example, a mule who is easy to handle in an arena can be hard on a trail. You must test the animal out alone. Sometimes, the mule will behave perfectly in the presence of a certain persona or his companions. When he is alone, he will showcase several behavioral quirks. There are several instances when a mule will be perfectly fine for a few miles away from his home. After that, they tend to turn back and run.

- You must never buy a mule that the seller is fond of. You should look for one that you like.

- In case the mule has been registered, you must make sure that all the documents of registration are in order before you buy the mule. You must never let them send you the papers later. Exchange money only when you have the papers in hand. You will also need a transfer form along with the complete registration paperwork. You must make copies of these documents once you receive them.

- The terms of sale should be clear. There are several issues that can arise with lawsuits. You must never take someone's "word for it" when it comes to buying livestock. If the mule turns out to be different from what you were told, your seller is less likely to return the money to you unless the terms are written on paper. A sales guarantee that lists your responsibilities and the seller's responsibilities should be signed by both parties to avoid any untoward incident.

While these are a few points of consideration, there are no rules when it comes to buying a mule. You need to use your common sense and have a lot of self-control to avoid any impulsive purchases that may lead to unpleasant experiences for you as well as the mule. That said, there will be pitfalls once the mule is brought home and you must be prepared to deal with them instead of abandoning the animal. Take as much time as you need before you finalize on the mule. Be sure to review as many mules as possible before you are able to take the final call on which one suits your home.

Chapter 3: Preparing For The Mule

Your farm should be equine friendly before you bring home a mule. From proper pasture conditions, adequate shelter to secure fencing, you should make sure everything is in place before the mule arrives. Doing this after you have brought the mule home will only spell trouble.

1.Getting the pasture ready

The area of the pasture is the first thing that you must consider. Each mule will require between 0.4 hectares per individual. This requirement depends upon the conditions of the ground, the season, the type of grass on the pasture and the pasture management efforts from your end. Now, if you have a smaller area, it is alright as long as your mule is housed in the shelter principally and uses the grazing areas occasionally.

You will need to employ a good pasture management program to ensure that the mules do not over graze and to also ensure that you are able to control worms, provide good drainage and also control the growth of weeds. Good pasture management includes activities like removal of the droppings, regularly rotating of the grazing area and preventing the mule from entering any wet muddy area.

Pasture safety
There are several types of plants that are toxic to mules, donkeys and horses. These should be removed from the area to keep the animal safe. Ragwort, for instance is very toxic. Any ingestion can lead to severe damage in the liver. It is a good idea to read pasture guides about removal and control of ragwort weed. These plants when merely cut, remain toxic to mules. You will have to remove them completely and also dispose of them correctly.

You must also remember that every part of this weed is poisonous for humans as well. So, gloves must be worn when you are pulling or cutting the weed.

Even pulling is not enough in case of flowering ragwort plants. You can consult a professional to help you effectively remove the weed. One of the best options is incineration or controlled burning. There are other plants such as laburnum and yew that are toxic to mules. You must make sure that they do not have access to these plants in any form.

Grass cuttings are also not advisable for mules and they should be kept away from garden waste of any kind.

Lastly, you need to remove any object that can cause injuries to your mule. Any sharp projections or unstable objects that may injure the animal should be removed immediately. Levelling the ground on a regular basis also prevents a lot of injuries in case of mules walking around free range. This prevents stumbling and any bone or muscle injury to the animal.

2. Fencing the area

There are several fencing options when it comes to mules. You will have to choose one that is safest for your pet based on the surroundings of your pasture and the possible threats to your mule. Here are the four most popular options:

Board fences

These fences are also called rail fences, plank or post fences that are very popular on farms because they look really nice. They are very easily visible to the animal and they are quite safe. These fences have treated wood planks that are sometimes also painted, that are screwed on to wooden posts. They may also be made of wooden rails that fit into slots on wooden posts or can be constructed from PVC plastic posts and boards. The biggest advantage with this type of fencing is that they are very economical. When maintained properly, they can last for about 25 years easily.

The wooden planks are most often made from oak that is treated and rough cut. With rough cut oak, you have the advantage of a rustic appearance. Oak is also a sturdy material that will remain intact even if an animal leans on it. The good thing is that mules do not like to chew on planks made of oak.

What you need to watch out for is warping of the board when it is freshly cut. In case there are any spots on the plank that have been weakened naturally, it may lead to quick rotting of the fence. Oak rots faster than any other type of wood. With treated pine, you have a good finish and even takes up paint quite well, although not easily. When treated, pine does not rot very easily. It also keeps mules away and discourages chewing. You have to keep up the treatment regularly as it can wear off. Since pine is not too strong, you will have to opt for thicker boards.

Vinyl fences

You can use solid PVC plastic to make fences. They are a lot more expensive than the wooden planks. This is because they require painting. However, in terms of maintenance, they cost a lot less to maintain.

You also have the option of vinyl dipped fences that consist of wooden planks that are dipped in vinyl. This is not as durable as the chance of warping is still high. In the southern states, mildew is a problem if you have white fencing.

Cattle Panels
Also known as stock panels, these are fabricated mesh fences that are usually made from galvanized steel. The rods are about ¼ inch in width. These fences are about 52 inches in height and have panels that are 8 inches thick.

The close set horizontal wires are tighter at the bottom to ensure that the smaller livestock do not escape. This is also extremely useful in keeping small predators out of your pasture. You can trim the panels as required as they come in rolls that are 16 feet in length. All you need is a heavy bolt cutter.

You also have sheep panels that are about 40 inches in height. The wires in this case are set closer to one another. The best type of panels are the utility panels that are extremely tough. They are made using 4 inch spacing and extra heavy duty 4-6 gauge rods. They are usually 20 feet in length and between 4-6 feet in height.

These panel fences are best to make stout corrals that last long, are economical and maintenance free. You have to be very cautious about the raw ends of the rod in each panel. They can be very sharp and can cause serious damage to your mule. You need to make sure that you smoothen out each sharp end using a rasp to take off the razor sharp edge.

Woven wire fences
Also known as a field fence or a wire mesh, a woven wire fence is one of the best options for a large area. They are made with several lines of smooth wire that is held apart using a stay, which is a vertical wire.

The spacing between these horizontal wires is close at the bottom. Usually the woven wire meshes are about 6 inches apart and have stays that are 12 inches long.

The biggest disadvantage with these fences is that they can be extremely expensive. However, in terms of security, they are the best. That is why they are great to mark the boundary of your pasture.

Most predators will be kept at bay when you use the wire fencing. They are about four feet in height and are ideal for all equines, especially miniature mules. If required, you can also install an electric wire above the fence for additional safety.

You can check the quality of the wire with the help of a few numbers that are printed on it. For example, if your fence reads 10-47-6-9, it means that the fence has 10 horizontal wires that have 6 inch spacing between them. The height is 47 inches and the wire used is a 9 gauge wire.

If you want a high tensile wire, it is more expensive than the standard ones. However, it will not rust or sag over time. It is also a lot lighter in weight.

These woven wires come with aluminum or zinc wiring. The coating is classified as Class I, II or III. Class III denotes the thickest coating. The higher the number, the more durable the fencing.

Kinds of fencing to avoid
In the year 1999, a fence safety survey was conducted by the Equine research Center in Guelph, Canada. This test was based on 180 horse owners who also owned donkeys and mules. On the positive side, 73% of these owners revealed that they had no injuries in the past year with their animals. However, with the remaining 27%, it was noted that the injuries were mostly fence related. Some of the injuries were so bad that the animal required veterinary care immediately. Here are some pointers that will help you understand the situations in which injuries are high:

- Barbed wired accounted for almost 63% of the injuries. The woven and high tensile wires were responsible for most serious injuries.

- The safest were the diamond mesh woven wires that caused about 6% of the injuries reported but none of them were serious.

- The board fences caused injuries in horses mostly as they ran into the fence or kicked them too hard. None of these injuries involved a mule, however.

- Injuries were reported with electrical tape. But these were only minor injuries.

- Interestingly, when a new animal was added to an established herd, it led to injuries. When the pastures were overcrowded, there were instances of the animals running in to the fences.

One of the most common options for fencing is the barbed wire. This is considered the ideal stockman's fence. However, the injuries caused by them have been extremely nasty as a mule can run into it. If you already have barbed wire around your property, it is a good idea to put another type of fencing that will be placed in front of the barbed wire. If you can replace the barbed wire with a type of fencing that is mule friendly, it is the best option available.

If you are choosing electric fencing, then make sure that the voltage is controlled. Should the mule run into it, he should only have a small jolt. Electric fences can be dangerous if you do not maintain them properly. They can be fatal for your animal in most cases.

The safest of all fences are the PVC fences. In the study conducted above, no injuries were reported because of them. So, if you are looking for the most reliable option for your pasture, investing in a good quality PVC fence can be a great idea.

The height of the fence is also an important factor in determining the effectiveness of it. Now, if you have a herd of mules, you will have to measure the height up to the withers of the tallest mule. The fence should be higher than this in order to be effective. This will also keep predators like coyotes at bay.

Lastly, make sure that the visibility of the fence is high. Use thicker wires, brighter color etc. so that your animal is able to view it from a distance. That will prevent them from running into it and injuring themselves. Although this is an uncommon occurrence with mules, taking precautions is the responsibility of the owner.

3.Housing mules

Proper shelters are extremely important for your mule. When the weather is not suitable or if the animal wants to simply rest, having good housing is a must. There are three things that you must consider when it comes to the shelter of the mule:

- It should be free from the risk of catching fire.
- It should have adequate ventilation and drainage.
- There should not be any risk of injury due to poor construction.

When you are planning a housing area for your mule, here are the things that you must consider:

Constructing the shelter

The construction should ensure that there are no projections on the surface of the stable or the shelter to prevent injury. You must clean all the exposed surfaces and disinfect them to ensure good health of your herd. If you are using treated wood or any paint on the surface of the construction material, it should not be toxic to mules. Wooden material requires preservatives to prevent any chance of rotting or warping.

The flooring should be levelled as much as possible and must not be slippery. Good drainage is necessary to make sure that any stable waste is drained out.

The doors should be at least 4 ft. wide. The height should be such that the mule is able to look out over the door by placing his head out. Use bolts on the top and bottom to make sure that the door is fastened well when the mules are inside. You can even have a top door that can be secured when in the open position. The disadvantage with a top door is that ventilation and sunlight is reduced when it is closed.

The stable should also have good lighting to ensure that the mule can see. Even the keeper will be able to examine the animal and handle them safely. You can have portable lighting as well. If you do plan to install the lighting inside the shelter, make sure that the bulbs are out of the mule's reach. The cabling should be secure and of high quality to prevent any chance of fires or short circuits.

The air circulation should be adequate while ensuring that there are no drafts inside the shelter. You can even install safety glass with each window to keep the shelter warm. It is best to keep one window open at all times unless the temperature drops drastically.

If you do not provide enough ventilation, there are chances that your mule will develop respiratory issues. While air flow should be kept at a maximum, you need to keep a constant check on the dust that is entering the stable.

Ideally the size of the shelter should be large enough to provide 10ftX12ft for each mule. This will allow them to rise easily, turn around while inside the stable and also maintain a safe distance from the other mules that you may have housed inside the stable. If you have a communal stable that houses a herd, space should be the top priority.

Proper bedding
Keeping your mules warm is very important. For this, adequate bedding material is necessary. This not only provides warmth but also protects the animal against any chance of injury. When the mule lies down on the floor, he will be comfortable with good bedding.

The bedding material should be free from mold and too much dust. The material should also be non-toxic to mules. The best option is rubber matting as it is also absorbent by nature. You can even add material like straw, shavings and other material that can absorb any urine. This material should be changed regularly and well managed to ensure complete hygiene and disease prevention.

Ensuring fire safety

The biggest risk in any stable is fire. You will have to take into consideration all the fire safety recommendations that are made in the "Guide to Fire Safety in Animal Establishments and Stables" laid out by your Local Government.

If you are unsure, you can also seek advice from a Fire Prevention Officer in your locality to understand the statutory requirements. If you have any combustible liquid or material in the barn, it should be removed instantly. You should also make sure that you do not smoke in the stable or in the areas near it.

The fire extinguishers, alarm systems and other equipment should be checked on a regular basis by someone who is qualified. If you have any electrical installation in the barn, it should be periodically inspected and maintained. The fittings and wires should not be accessible to the mules.

You must also make sure that it is earthed properly and is kept safe from any rodent. If you need to use extension cables and leads, you should make sure that it does not get entangled in the legs of the animal, leading to serious injuries.

Metal pipe work and any steel that is used in the structure should be earthed well. You can take additional precaution by ensuring that all the installations are protected by an RCD or a residual current device.

Lastly, in case there is an outbreak of a fire, you should make sure that your animals can be released easily. A fire exit should be installed and an emergency turnout procedure should be planned and communicated to everyone who is working at the stable with the mules.

Adding rugs

Not all mules need rugs for protection. They are hardy creatures. If they have thick coats, they are additionally equipped to survive harsh winters. However, if the mule is old, clipped or is not as hardy, you have to keep him protected from any draft or low temperature. You can also use these rugs to keep flies at bay. Any turnout rug should be removed in case the weather improves to prevent the stable from getting very warm.

The size of the hood and the rug should be good enough to suit the size of the mule. You need the right size to ensure that there are no abrasions, hair loss or restricted movements. They should be removed on a regular basis to check the body condition of the mule. You should also make sure that the mule does not get too hot because of the rug being on him constantly.

The rugs should be cleaned and repaired regularly. In case of any wetness in the rugs, you should have a spare one that you can use on your mule. These precautions ensure that the animal stays clear of any illnesses.

Tethering
Securing the animal using a chain or any kind or anchorage is called tethering. With this, you are able to confine the mule in an area that you want him to stay in. Long term management is not possible with tethering. This makes the animal incapable of exercising himself and even restricts freedom to a large extent.

You must also consider the possibility of injuries related to entangling of the legs. In addition to that, the animal becomes incapable of escaping predators as well.

Short term tethering, however, can be very useful. If you need to restrict food intake for medical reasons, for instance, tethering becomes important. So, you need to provide some facility where the mule can be tethered in case of such an emergency.

In case you decide to have your mule tethered, you need to remember that he should be checked on every six hours. That way, you will be aware of any requirement that your mule may have, such as water or food. You may also have to tether your mule in order to manage an orthopedic condition.

Chapter 4: Bringing The Mule Home

Once the mule is home, taking care of the animal is entirely your responsibility. You should make sure that you give the donkey everything that he needs in order to be safe and healthy. From feeding to making sure that he is introduced to the other animals and your family correctly will go a long way in keeping your pet happy.

1.Introducing mules to household pets

Mules are known to be gentler with household pets than donkeys. This is mainly because they are not easily startled which makes them behave less impulsively when approached by a pet.

If you have a pet dog or cat at home and want your mule to mix with them, it may not be the best idea. Now, instinctively, mules are guard animals that are meant to ward off canine predators and other predators. So, in all probability, your mule will consider your pet a threat to his well-being or the well-being of his companions.

The mule is a docile creature, no doubt. But, at the same time, you must never underestimate the power of a mule. All it really takes is one kick for your dog to be severely injured. In some cases, the kick can also be a threat to your dog's life. Now, that said, you do not have to completely drop the idea of bringing a mule home if you have a pet dog or cat. Here are some options that you can try:

- Keep them in separate areas even on the pasture: You can have a portable fence that the mules can stay in when your dogs are out. This is a very important measure if you see any aggression from the dogs towards the mule or vice versa. In most cases, a well-trained dog will be easy to handle even without the fence as long as you are supervising the interactions.

  The fence is a good option for introductions. You can keep the animals separated by a portable fence and watch their body language. Any discomfort or unnecessary excitement will become obvious to you. When you see the dog and the mule oblivious to each other's presence, you can safely let them out of the fence but only when they are under supervision.

- Work on training your pets: Just like dogs, mules can also be trained for obedience commands like recall. This is very important when you have mixed animal species in your pasture. Similarly, you have to train the dog well, too. If your dog is not fully trained or is still a puppy, you must always keep him away from the mule unless you are confident that they are completely in your control.

If you are looking for guard animals on a farm for your livestock, then having mules and dogs on the farm is a great idea. You see, mules are able to keep most predators away. However, with some predators like bob cats or jungle cats, dogs are able to handle them a lot better.

The best precaution you can take is to select a mule with a calm temperament when you have other pets at home. You must always be aware of the fact that there is a small amount of risk when you are placing these animals in one area. So, in case of any accident or untoward incident, you must remember never to blame the mule or the dog. They always react out of their instincts and never cause any harm or damage intentionally. If you want your pets to be safe, taking complete precaution is your responsibility.

2.Introducing mules to children

The good news for all mule owners is that mules are naturally conditioned to being great around children. In most cases, homes that have kids would prefer a miniature mule who will be easier to handle and can even make a wonderful ride for the kids every once in a while.

That said, you must never forget that even with a very gentle mule, you are dealing with an instinctive being. You have to learn and teach your child how to approach the mule to ensure that they are completely safe. Here are a few tips that will help:

- Never startle the animal. Tell your child never to shout or scream when they are approaching the animal. It is natural for a child to be excited when they see a furry creature and they tend to make loud noises of approval. While you know that the child is excited, the mule is going to respond to the sound.

- Always approach the animal slowly. Children tend to run towards an animal and embrace them by the muzzle. This is dangerous if the temperament of the mule is not entirely known to you. It is best that you silently and calmly approach the mule.

- The best thing to do would be to stand at a distance from the mule with the child and wait for the mule to approach you. If he is calm and the ears are flat to the side, then it means that the mule is relaxed. If you see that the ears drop down and are flipped back, you must never approach the mule. This is his warning sign to you that he does not like what is going on at that moment. Mules can be vicious in the fight mode and you must never let a child approach him.

- You need to learn to interact with the animal first. Before you can introduce the child to the mule without any physical barrier, you should know exactly how to approach a mule safely. If you have doubts about this, it is a risk to let your child into the mule's space.

- Let the child accompany you in routine activities like feeding and filling the water troughs. This is the safest way to get the mule to become aware of the presence of the child and also learn the scents associated with you and your entire family.

The only time that a mule and a child may have a confrontation is if you fail to educate the child about properly dealing with the mule. Most human beings, adults included, often fall short when it comes to interacting with other species.

You have to inform your child that verbal communication does not mean anything to the animal. So kind words does not mean that the mule will be friendly towards you. Use little verbal communication and try to deal with the animal calmly. Teaching your child this skill will make them have safe and enjoyable interactions with the mule. However, you must never leave a child unsupervised when a mule is around.

3. What to feed mules

Mules are among the lowest maintenance equines. They are a lot easier and more economical when it comes to the food requirements. In comparison to donkeys as well, the mule tends to be easier to feed. In this section you will learn about what you can feed donkeys and how you can occasionally give them treats as well.

When you are feeding a mule, the first thing you should remember is that the mule is not similar to the horse in any way. Their food requirements resemble the dietary needs of donkeys more closely. They have entirely different physiology and digestion. The metabolism of these creatures is drastically different too.

Horses require a high calorie diet that is of very high quality. Giving your mule this food can actually be hazardous to his health! If you do not provide your mule with the right kind of food, he may become obese and may develop ailments related to the hoof and important body organs such as the liver. A mule who does not get good food will never live his normal life span which is about 15-30 years depending upon the quality of life that they get.

In addition to this, you should also understand that the mule is unlike the cow, sheep or other ruminant and should never be fed like one.

Water

Mules require continuous supply of water all day. If you cannot supply fresh water continuously, you should make sure that they have enough clean water to drink. This is imperative to ensure that their welfare needs are taken care of.

Even if you have a pasture that is surrounded by natural sources of water such as streams, rivers or ponds, it is not satisfactory as the water is usually contaminated. In this case, you have to look for an alternate source of water.

If you have a water source, make sure that it is well maintained. Now, the sources containing a sandy base are not recommended as they cause a lot of problems for the mule. Another important point with natural sources of water is that they get icy cold in winters. During the hot months as well, you have to look for alternate sources of water as it may get too hot for the mule to go outside.

The water buckets and troughs have to be fixed at a convenient height securely. If you have mules of different sizes, then the water troughs should be placed properly. In many cases, mules that cannot reach the trough will try to paw the water. That way, the chances of the trough getting dislodged increase. This can lead to serious injuries. Keep a check on the water containers to make sure that they are always full.

If your mules are stabled they will need a lot more access to fresh water. You can opt for automatic waterers but ensure that you check them regularly to ensure that they are working properly.

Maintenance of the water container is a must. Make sure that it is cleaned regularly. Preventing the build-up of any algae or debris is mandatory. Do not use cleaning substances that may be toxic to the animal.

If your mule is tethered, you have to refill the water troughs on a regular basis. The water trough should be easy to clean and should be spill proof to ensure that the water does not spill if there is any entangling with the tether.

Mules require a lot of water each day. They will need between 25-50 liters depending upon the size of the body. The consumption of water increases in the warmer months. You will also have to take into consideration the changing water requirements. For instance, lactating mares will need a lot more water.

Grass
If your mules are free range, then they will browse around and consume the amount of water that they need. Usually a mule will need a rotated, mixed pasture that is about ½ an acre in area.

Since the mule is similar to the donkey in food requirements, they will consume dry grass and also feed from small bushes just like the donkey in the natural environment. They cannot, however, thrive only on grass. Grass does not have the necessary nutrients and is also too high in moisture content.

You need to make sure that your mule does not graze or get pasture time when the grass may be more moisture laden. This includes the early mornings and the frosty time of the year. You also need to make sure that they do not consume too much spring grass as it is too rich for the metabolism of the mule. If your pasture has very good growth of grass, you need to monitor the movement of the mule.

Consuming too much grass does have a flipside. It can lead to obesity, hoof problems and also colic pain in the mule. Grass cuttings should never be given to a mule as the resulting colic pain can be fatal.

If you are unable to manage the movement of the mule, you can make use of portable electric fences. That will help you manage the pasture and also restrict the areas that the mule will move around in. Another way to control the grazing of your mule is to mow the area before allowing the mule to graze. This is very important to manage the sugar levels in your mule's body. In addition to that, you can also control the parasitic worms that may affect the health of the animal.

Barley straw and grass hay
The requirement of a dry and high fiber diet of your mule can be managed with the help of grass hay. This should be a staple in your mule's diet throughout the year.

Hay should be included in the diet when the pasture is too rich, moist or lush. Mules require low protein diets which can be fulfilled with the help of grass hay in the diet. You must not provide your mule with any alfalfa hay as it has about 25% protein content that can actually be too high for your mule.

Grass hay also helps maintain the dental health of your mule. Since the hay needs to be chewed well for the animal to consume it, the teeth stay in good condition. That way the necessary nutrients are also released properly. If your mule is unable to chew the hay properly and digest it, it is the indication of poor dental health that needs to be rectified at the earliest for overall health benefits.

On an average, an adult mule who will measure about 230 kilos will need to consume close to 2% of their body weight's equivalent of hay in a day. It depends on the season as well, with the consumption being lowered in the warmer months.

A mule who is healthy will eat all day long. So, you need to ensure that you match the appetite of the mule with food that is low in energy value. That way, you prevent your pet from getting too obese.

Your mule should have access to a generous quantity of grass hay or barley straw of good quality. You can provide this with the help of a hay net or any other suitable container.

The daily ration of hay or barley straw should be divided into 2 or 3 servings per day. That way they have access to high fiber and low calorie forage all day. Barley straw should be the primary feed. You can also use oat straw if the mule is old or underweight.

In case of the younger mules that have better teeth, you can use wheat stray that is more fibrous but much lower in the energy value.

Salt and mineral blocks
Mules need a lot of trace minerals and salts. This can be provided with mineral blocks that are specially designed for the equines. You can place the block in a special container that is designed for it. You can also place it near the water trough. Now, it is important that you do not give your mule salt blocks that are made for cattle. These are rich in urea that is very unhealthy for a mule.

Treats
Now every pet owner wants to spoil his or her pet with a lot of treats and goodies. You can certainly do the same with your mule. However, the treats that you give your mule should not be too high in calories and carbs. This leads to digestive issues as well as hoof diseases.

You must avoid lawn clippings and breads that have very high levels of starches and carbohydrates that are unhealthy. You must also limit the amount of treats that you give your mule.

If your mule is constantly expecting treats, he will become very agitated and may develop issues like biting if they do not like the treat that they are receiving. One of the best treats to give your mule is carrots. Cut them lengthwise and offer them to ensure that your mule does not choke on them.

Eating habits of your mule must be monitored carefully. These animals will not show any signs of pain or illness. However, they will give you warning signs in the form of a noticeable change in the appetite. If you notice any sudden change, make sure that you consult your vet.

Healthy feeding tips
- Make sure that the food that you give your mule is good in quality. It should be free from any debris, soil or poisonous plants. The food must be visibly free from any dust or mold.

- It is a good idea to feed the mule at floor level. That keeps their respiratory system in good condition. However, the ground that you feed them on should be very clean.

- The food that you give your mule should be stored in containers that are vermin proof. That way, it will not spoil easily. You can also ensure that the feeding quality is maintained.

- The feeding container that you use should be kept very clean to prevent any infestation with rodents or vermin. Any remaining food should be cleaned out every day. Each feed should be prepared freshly and should be mixed well.

- In case you are feeding a group of mules at once, you must give each mule an individual feeder. The distance between each feeder should be equivalent to two mules' length. That way, you will prevent any risk of food related competition that can cause fights among your mules.

On a regular basis, make sure that you are monitoring the weight of your mules. An increase in weight is an indication of impending obesity that can lead to a lot of metabolic issues in the mule.

If you are making any change in your diet in terms of the volume or the type of food you are providing, do it gradually. If the changes are too sudden, it will lead to colic pain and diarrhea in your mule.

If you are a first time mule owner, you should make sure that you consult your vet to understand the correct way to feed your mule. An equine vet or nutritionist will be able to assess the requirements of your mule and suggest a diet according to the age and weight.

4.Grooming a mule

It is important to groom a mule in order to ensure that the coat stays smooth and shiny. If you plan to enter your mule into shows, grooming is particularly important. Mules will grow a lot of wooly fur during winters that needs to be trimmed and maintained in order to keep him looking clean and healthy.

Trimming the mule

Now, the mane, the ears, tail and the underjaw will have a lot of hair that will make the mule look shabby. You will have to trim this hair to give him a smooth appearance.

You can use scissors to trim the excess hair. You need to make sure that you have scissors with rounded ends to give the mule a good trim. You can also use dog clippers and razor blades to cut the excess hair. Here are some trimming tips that you need to keep in mind:

- **The jawline:** The long hair from the chin up to the jowl is should be trimmed gently. This needs to be done to prevent your mule from looking like the head just extends into the neck without a proper demarcation. While doing this, remember to get a smooth outline.

- **The mane:** You will need to separate any brown or grey hair that is growing from the neck from the darker strands of hair. You will start trimming near the withers and first cut the pale colored hair. The mane must be cut on either side while ensuring that you do not cut too close to the skin. After you have evenly shortened the hair on both sides, you can cut the rest of the mane to the size that you desire. Hold the hair that you want to cut off between the index finger and the second finger just as a barber would. Then. You can trim the area just behind the ears to make the saddle fit properly.

- **Ears:** It can be a task to cut the hair on the ears as mules hate when their ears are touched. You need to be very patient with this. Start by stroking the ear from the base to the tip. When the mule is relaxed, you can cup the edges of the ear to move the hair forward. Cut the tips of the hair to level with the edge. You can then trim any hair around the edges.

- **Tail:** The first thing that you need to do is detangle the hair on the tail. This can be done by just running your finger through the hair of the tail. You can then use a comb to smoothen it out even more. Trim the hair just below the hocks by about 4 inches. Place your hand under the tail, lift it and then cut at an angle. The top section should be trimmed so that the stubby short hair is removed right to the root of the tail.

- **Hooves:** You will not see any feathers around the hooves in most mules. However, if you trim any long hair that may be growing over the face of the hoof, you will get it looking a lot cleaner. The lower legs can be left without trimming if you are not too skilled. This hair growth will fall out on its own after winter is over.

- **Tummy hair:** The tummy hair, too, will fall out eventually. If you groom the mule every day and brush him, especially, this hair will not be a problem. Avoid trimming it using a scissor as you will leave scissor marks everywhere. In the case of the younger mules, leaving the tummy hair is a good idea, as it will give the appearance of great depth in the body that is actually not present.

Trimming the mule on a regular basis will also help you keep a check on lice that is a common issue with equines.

Bathing a mule

Lice are extremely common in mules, as mentioned above. Giving your mule an anti-lice bath can prevent the occurrence of these parasites. Along with clipping, bathing is a good option to keep your mule well groomed. It is good to bathe your mule after you have clipped off any excess fur. That way, the disinfecting shampoo will reach the skin of the mule.

Adult lice actually drown when you bathe the mule. The lice can pose a threat which is why you should bathe the mule regularly so that the ones that have hatched can be washed away. Eventually you will reach a stage when the existing eggs have hatched but the adults have been removed before they can lay more eggs.

You may ask your vet to suggest a good anti lice shampoo. If that is unavailable, you can use a baby shampoo that is mild and perfume free. That way, the eyes and the skin of the mule will not be harmed.

You can follow these steps to bathe your mule safely:

- Make sure that you use lukewarm water unless the weather is very hot. When you are bathing your mule you have to take a lot of time during which you have to constantly reassure the animal.

- You will need a lot of watering cans and sprinkler heads in order to hose the mule down with warm and cold water alternatively.

- You will also need two sponges to clean the face and the ears.

- It is a good idea to have someone along with you to assist you when you are bathing the mule.

- To start the bath, fill a bucket with warm water. Make sure that you have the right temperature. If the water is too hot or cold, it will startle the mule.

- The body should be wet all over except for the head and the ears. You must pour the water over the animal slowly and avoid drenching him in one go. If this the first bath, remember that it is a strange sensation for the mule.

- Take a small amount of the shampoo and massage it on to the body. The more shampoo you use, the harder it will be to rinse it off.

- Begin from the neck and work your way down. Pay attention to the mane, the armpits, the withers and the groin. These are the areas with maximum lice infestation.

- Then wet the face and the areas just behind the ears with the sponge. Cover the eyes with your hand while you do this.

- You can squeeze a small amount of shampoo on the sponge and work it on the skin in these areas.

- Rinse the whole body thoroughly using clean warm water. You can use a cup or a clean sponge over the ears and the face of the mule. You must be very careful not to get any water into the eyes of the mule.

- Dab the body dry with large towels. You will need the smaller ones for the ears and the face.

Once your mule has been bathed, praise him immensely and reward him. You can use a ginger biscuit as a special bath time reward. Make sure that all the grooming tools and the bathing material that you use is washed completely after the bath. That way, you can ensure that it is safe to be used for the next bath.

Remember to keep calm when you do this and take it slow. Never make sudden changes in your interaction with the mule or you will scare him.

5. Keeping the stable clean

If you have younger mules on your farm, you need to know that they have a very sensitive respiratory system. If you are unable to maintain the stable in good condition, it will lead to a lot of health issues in the mule. Here are a few stable management tips that will help you keep the stable clean and tidy.

- **Wear the right clothes:** While you are cleaning the stable, wearing the right clothes can save you a lot of time and can also prevent injuries. Start by wearing gloves that will protect you from blisters. Wearing rubber shoes will save you a lot of time that may otherwise be spent in cleaning the shoes.

- **Clear out the area that is to be cleaned:** Get your mule out of the stable or shelter. The best time to clean the stable is when your mule is grazing in the pasture. You need to get all the feeding and watering troughs out of the way. If you are unable to get your mule to stay outside, you can tether him temporarily while you clean up the stall.

- **Get your tools in place:** You will need a large wheel barrow in order to collect all the muck that you are likely to rake out of the stable of your mule. A pitch fork or a shovel is also necessary to do a thorough cleaning job with the stable.

- **Dig out the muck:** If the bedding consists of hay, you will need a pitchfork to rake it all out. In case you are using sawdust or shavings, you will need a shavings fork. The wet bedding and manure should be removed to ensure that the stable is clean. You can fork everything out into the wheel barrow. Take out small portions so that it becomes easy for you to push the wheel barrow around. Choose a dedicated manure pile where you can drop off all the muck you raked out.

- **Even the area:** Once you have removed all the wet bedding and manure, the clean bedding should be spread over the floor just as before. You should make sure that bedding is distributed evenly. Make sure you check the edges to ensure that the middle is not thinner than the sides.

The new bedding should be fluffed out using the pitch fork. You can even buy compacted shavings if you need to refill the area with clean bedding. The thickness of the bedding will be determined by the flooring and the season. If the weather is cold, you will have to add a thicker layer of bedding. Also the harder the floor, the thicker the bedding. If the floor is made of rubber matting, for instance, you will not need a thick layer of bedding to go with it.

- **Weekly cleaning schedule:** Having a weekly maintenance schedule can work wonders in reducing your burden of cleaning the area. It is a good idea to remove the wet or soiled bedding on a weekly basis to keep it from getting smelly. Using a stable disinfectant is a good idea. Make sure that the floor is fully dry before you put any bedding back on it.

Once you have completed the cleaning ritual, you need to sweep up any residual manure that may have spilled when cleaning. You can also dust the alleys and doors to get rid of dust and cobwebs. That way, you are assured of through cleaning of the stable area.

Always collect the manure and dirt in a designated area. Simply pushing it to the doorway will leave a muddy mess when the rains come in.
That may increase the chances of diseases and germs.

Chapter 5: Bonding With Your Mule

Mules crave companionship. When you take the time out to form a good bond with your mule, you will certainly have a great companion for life. These highly intelligent creatures require someone who can lead them in the right direction and convince them that they need to follow certain rules before they do.

This chapter will teach you how you can gain the trust of your mule and train them in ways that are most beneficial to them and to you.

1.Understanding your mule's body language

The first step towards building a relationship with your mules is being able to communicate with them. In the case of all pets, verbal communication is the least important tool. What you must focus on mostly is the body language. That will help you figure out the mood and the emotions that your pet is trying to convey. That will make training a lot easier.

Approaching a mule

Communication can be initiated only when you are able to approach your pet confidently without causing any panic or negative experience for either of you. Even when you have a mule who has been trained, you need to be cautious when you are approaching him. Here are a few tips to approach a mule properly:

- Make sure that you start slow. Walk towards the mule slowly and keep the talking to a minimum. The only thing the mule will focus on is your body and the signals that you are giving out.

- Stop at regular intervals and observe the mule. Does he want to approach you himself? Or is he trying to get away from you? If he is moving away, you must stand quietly and let him relax.

- After a few moments have elapsed, try to approach the mule again. Make sure that your hands are lowered. Your mule may want to smell your hand. That is normal. If you hold the hand up, it might seem like a threat to the mule who will think that you are going to strike him.

- When you get close, your mule might try to sniff at you for sometime. The scent that you emit is one of the most important things for the mule. This is the first association with a human that the mule will make. So, be as calm as possible and make sure that you do not startle the animal.

Signals with the ear
The ears of a mule are a powerful tool of communication. Here are some signals that he is trying to give you with the ears:

- If both the ears are facing forward, then the mule is focusing on something behind you. He may also be trying to understand your movement to figure out where you are trying to go.

- One ear forward and the other back. This is an indication of extreme curiosity. He is trying to listen for different sounds in the environment while understanding what you want from him.

- Ears to the side, resting flat means that the mule is relaxed. This is when it is safest to approach the animal.

- Both ears up, facing back. This means that the mule is aware of some activity that is going on behind him. However, he is still watching you.

- The ears are back and facing down. This is a warning signal that tells you that the mule is extremely uncomfortable. When you see this ear position, do not approach the mule at any cost.

Signaling with general body language
There are a few things that your mule will do with his body after you have successfully approached him. Some may be signs of inviting you while others are telling you to back away.

- The mule nudges you to tell you to get out of the way. You may be standing in the way of a toy or some food that he is eating.

- He makes a nipping action with the mouth. This is a sign of warning. The mule is telling you that he does not approve of you being too close to him.

- Keeping one leg raised. In case the mule is eating, this means that he is fully focused on this activity. You must not approach a mule in this state as he may get startled and react in an unexpected manner.

- He pulls at your sleeve. This means that the mule wants something that you have with you. If this habit is not stopped, it can lead to a painful bite in the future. You must stop this with a strong "No". The voice must be loud and abrupt.

- He rests his head on your shoulder. This is a sign that the mule is very comfortable in your presence. A mule in this state is comfortable with you approaching him.

- He turns around and places his hind towards you. This is a sign that he is extremely nervous. When the mule does this do not pet the animal. He might be getting ready to kick the person approaching him. This can lead to severe injuries if you get too close to the animal.

- Switching of the tail. This is a signal that the mule is clearly annoyed with something. You must look around when he does this. If you cannot find anything around you, reexamine your action and movement. If it is too swift or sudden, your mule will not be too comfortable.

How to use verbal communication
While it is true that mules do not respond first to verbal communication, it is not obsolete. The tone of your voice is very important and not so much the words that you use.

- Keeping the tone uniform during a certain movement allows your mule to read what it means. For instance, if you use the word regularly in a certain tone, he understands that you are not pleased with something.

- The level of the voice is important. If you keep the voice soft and low, it can have a rather calming effect on the mule.

Remember, while words are not really a method of communicating with animals, the tone is universal. But, without any control on your body language and the energy that you are emitting, the tone of your voice cannot help you much when it comes to dealing with creatures that belong to another species. The cues that you give to the animal are of utmost importance.

2. Training the mule
Training a mule is not very different from training a horse. The major difference that you may notice is in the attitude and instinct of the animal. That will change your approach in various situations. The techniques, however, remain the same.

Imprinting
With a young foal, imprinting can have a lot of benefits. Imprinting is common with all equine foals. This is where you get the animal used to your touch, your voice, your smell and your energy. These things are usually taught to a foal by his mother. This will shape the character when he is older.

If you want him to be a trainable individual, you need to make sure that you teach him to be willing from the time he is born. If the mare chosen for your mule is calm in her temperament, it is likely that the mule will have the same disposition. When a mare gives birth to a young foal, she will teach him to behave in the same way. On the other hand, if the mare is difficult to handle, you may have trouble handling her foal.

When you begin to imprint the foal, have the goal for him clear. Basically, you need to know what attitude you want him to develop. Adopt the right approaching techniques and ensure that you provide him with a lot of patience and calmness. That is what he will learn from you.

If you respect the foal, you can demand respect from him. Set limitations with his behavior. If the foal was in a herd, the first thing that he is taught is to respect space. This is what you must try to teach him without being too overbearing. If the foal kicks, bites or misbehaves, you can give him a sharp pat on the side of the rump or the mouth.

At the same time, when the foal displays good behavior, do not forget to give him a good reward. That will foster a relationship between you that will last for a really long time.

Keep it fun
If learning becomes threatening or boring for the mule, he will learn very little. Make sure that it is a good balance between work and play. The more fun you make it, the more he will want to spend his time and be around you. Mules have an innate need to serve and please. This comes out with the individual he is imprinted with.

Never rush the response with a mule. If you have trained a horse before, you must not expect the same rate of response from the mule. With horses, a quick response is the norm. However, the bright side of training a mule is that while response is slow the memory and retention is much higher than a horse.

Starting from scratch
Whether you are training a foal or an adult, the one thing that you must keep in mind is to start from the basics. You will begin with imprinting and then take it to the basic routines.

The first thing that you will do is to put on a halter correctly. You can ask the ranch that you bought the mule from to assist you with this. Once you know that the mule is not bothered by the removing and putting on of the halter, you can proceed to tether him. After the halter has been placed, find a secure post to tether him to.

Leave him after tying him and come back after a few minutes. Then untie him and say the words, "Come". He may not step forward immediately. If that occurs, tie him again and leave. Try this every ten minutes. The moment he steps forward with you, give him a treat and praise him generously.

Stroking a mule on the neck and the shoulder will be appreciated a lot. You can even stroke the ears and the chest. Then you can try a few more steps. Don't force him to respond immediately. Try a few steps the first day and a few more after. That will make him lead easily.

Once you are able to lead the mule easily, walk him around the farm. You can introduce him to things like machines that may scare him when you begin the training process. A calm introduction will prevent fear in the future. Make sure you give your mule a lot of rewards as you walk along. The more you reward him, the easier he is going to be to lead.

Once you are able to walk, you can set up tiny obstacles or even choose obstacles around your farm and pasture. The best options are logs, bridges and tires. The mule may be unwilling to negotiate these obstacles initially. However, he will try when he is coaxed. Use a short lead and stand very close to the head. Then say the word, "Come" to pull him forward. The moment he is able to move one foot over the obstacle, stop right there and reward him. When he proceeds with the next foot, reward him again and so on. This obstacle course should be slow and easy. Don't rush through it.

What you need to bear in mind is that the mule will not walk straight on the obstacle. He may tend to become a little crooked. Then, you will walk in front of him. Be directly in front, hold his halter on either side and make him walk in a straight line.

The way to know if the basic training is successful is if the mule is able to walk with you on a slack lead easily. If he is resisting, be consistent and persistent in training. Keep stopping and starting till he is able to walk with you on a loose leash. That will also help you control the speed that he walks with. You can make him jog and trot on command with a loose leash.

The next way to know is that the mule will stand in place with the lead and halter. While you brush him, he will stand still and stay completely calm.

Advanced training
Mules can learn pretty much any verbal command that you may want to teach a dog. However there are some commands that will be beneficial to the mule and also to the owner when taught correctly.

Whoa

This is the command that you will use when you want the mule to stop. When you want him to stop just stop walking yourself and use the command "Whoa". If he complies, you can reward him. This is an important command if your mule is about to attack a family pet, is going to run into a fence or is in any dangerous situation.

Over

You want to train the mule to move over or turn around. This is a little hard as you have to approach him from the front and nudge him to do it. Unless your animal has complete trust in you, he will view this as a predatory move and may attack.

Take the mule into a training pen and let him relax and get familiar with the area. Then, step toward the shoulder and pull the head towards you. You can tap him on the flank and give him the verbal command of "Move over". You must not move with your body unless the mule is very reluctant to move.

The first thing the mule needs to learn is hindquarter control. That will only come when you are gentle with him. Take it one step at a time. If he crosses over the offside hind, give him a reward and encourage him to step more. For the first time you can stop at two steps. You can ask for few more steps with each session.

The next step is to get the shoulders away from you. This is harder as the front feet are usually glued hard on the floor. Hold the side of the halter and ask him to move over again. This time, give him a firmer tap. Use your body weight to bring him around if he does not comply immediately.

You can repeat this three times. If he does not comply, then you can give him a sharp tap on the shoulder once. He may just step over by surprise. That is when you will reward him very generously.

Back

The final and most important command is back. You will have to use the lead in the left hand and pull it back in a downward direction. Then release it while you say the command, "back". Normally, a mule will step back. If he doesn't, you can use the right hand to push at him at the middle of the chest and release. This works best when you use a single finger. You have to push him quite hard to get him to move the first time.

The moment he steps back, pet him and reward him. Repeat this not more than three times and complete the session. You can keep increasing the response each time.

With every verbal command, you can try three repetitions each time. Do not force him to do any more than that as he can get a little aggressive. Once he is able to comply well, you can improve the training by teaching him commands such as lunge. These commands take a lot of patience and will require your mule to have some trust in you to perform it perfectly.

Never train the mule in a hurry. You should be able to spend a lot of time together and make this a fun and enjoyable experience for the both of you. Fast forwarding training is never going to get you the response you want from the mule.

Training mules for riding
All of the commands mentioned above were with respect to handling the mule by the halter. Now, the next thing that you want to be able to do is ride the mule. First, you must have all the verbal commands in place, especially whoa and trot. If his ground drive during the walk is easy, you are ready to mount him. That is only possible if he is a mule that is large enough to ride.

Get him used to the idea of mounting. Mount from one side and dismount from the other and watch his reaction. If he is able to remain calm, then you have the opportunity to stay on his back for a while. After you sit on his back, hold a treat to his mouth and encourage him to move his head around a little to get the treat from you. While doing so, you can even tug at the halter and rein on the sides gently. This will give you the benefit of a light brindle when you begin to walk him. Your mule is fairly ready to move ahead with you still aboard. This will require an assistant initially.

Let the person with you lead the mule forward. Remember that both of you have to give the "Come" or "Walk Command". To give the mule a cue, you will have to squeeze the legs around the body. That is when your assistant will lead him on. A riding crop might be necessary if he does not comply at first.

After every few steps, use the "whoa" command. If he stops on command, give him a reward. Even if he has just walked two steps, it is a significant mark of progress. Continue this lesson till your mule has finished one complete rotation of the stable one way. Always remind him to stop with a "whoa" command. If your mule is good with the back-up command, you can ask him to do this as well.

You can give your mule a cue to stop as well. As you say "whoa", pull the reins gently. That will become a habit even without the verbal cue.

Back up can be taught to the mule by pulling the reins down and back. In case he does not comply with this in the first few attempts, you have the option of getting your assistant to push him back as you had done previously while teaching him the command. When you are pushing him back with the reins, watch his reaction. If he is jutting his head forward, it means that he is not happy doing it. If you persist too much he may have a negative response.

Remember that mules learn quite differently from horses. The response might be slower and a little frustrating at first. All you need to do is stay in tune with the person who is assisting you. Be very careful not to confuse the mule.

The next thing that you want to teach him is to trot with you aboard. This is not the easiest thing to do but it can be achieved. Riding with a mule is a great idea because of the temperament of the animal. He is less likely to get startled and bolt off. They are also willing to work with you for long periods of time after they have been trained. That said, if you have smaller sized mules, they tend to have the personality of a pony and will try their best to get away with stuff often.

Strength is the most important quality of a mule. They are able to carry some large weights on their body without even flinching a little. They are also a lot more surefooted, although there have been cases of stumbling in the past. The one thing you need to remember with the mule is that you must never lean forward as the speed picks up as you would do with a horse. This will throw him off balance. To be on the safer side, you must try to get the mule to move at fast speeds only when the route is somewhat levelled.

3. Jobs mules can perform

You can have a lot of fun with mules and they are great utility creatures as well. Once they are trained, they can perform a variety of tasks depending upon the breed that you are handling and the physical traits of each individual mule.

The personality of a mule is quite astonishing. They have the best pet qualities if you are able to spend a few hours training them and trying to get them used to you and your energy. Besides the fact that they can be wonderful companions, mules can perform several tasks routinely at the pasture. Here are a few things that you can use your mule for:

- **Sheep protection:** This task is usually presented to female mules. Males can become too aggressive with the sheep. You can introduce your mule to the herd using temporary fences. After a while, the single mule will form a bond with the herd. When this happens, the mule will protect the herd from any canine predator.

  If you have a pasture with sheep that are free ranging, then this is a huge advantage. The reason why people prefer to keep mules over guard dogs is that mules feed just like the sheep and you can have them feed and live together. With dogs you have to invest in their food separately.

  Mules can even live in the same area as the sheep. In case of any danger, the mule will also raise an alarm that will alert the sheep. In case of a predator attack, mules are known to chase the predator and trample him. This is not a common occurrence with miniature mules as they are too small to go after the predator.

- **Halter breaking:** A standard sized mule will also halter break the younger mules after they have been trained. The trained or older mule will sport a collar that is connected to the younger mule's halter. You can leave them out in the pasture under supervision.

  Lead training is an unpleasant task and when you let the mule train a younger one, the latter will not associate you with the negative experience. You will see that the foal who is released from the older mule will follow you very easily.

  You can get any breed of mule to perform this task for you. They are naturally attuned to training younger mules.

- **Foal companionship:** During the weaning stage, a mule can make a wonderful companion to foals of all equines. Let the mule run around the pasture with the mare before you wean a foal. Then when you are weaning a foal, you can leave the mule with him.

  A mule makes for a very calm companion. It also makes them very steady mentally. You will notice that the foal will actually turn to the mule for comfort. That reduces the stress caused by separation from the dam. Most mules are comfortable around people. This trait, too is transferred to the mule. So, when you bring home a mule companion for a foal, you reduce the stress of separation and also make the foal people friendly.

- **Stable companion:** This role is similar to providing companionship to the foal. Mules will actually take on the responsibility of improving the well-being of other animals. If you have a nervous horse in your stable you can introduce him to a mule who will make for a wonderful pasture and stall mate.

  You can also introduce the mule as a companion to a horse who is recovering from surgery or trauma. This is very useful for race horses who need to develop that calmness after an injury.

  The best mule for this purpose is the miniature mule as they do not take up much space but provide the same amount of positive energy to the animal.

- **Riding programs for the handicapped:** Time and time again, mules have proved that they can have a very positive effect on children and people who are disabled. In most parts of England the mule is promoted as an animal who can be in riding programs for the physically challenged.

  Since they are smaller in size and have a much calmer disposition, they are easy for them to ride. Mules are very thoughtful and can be extremely affectionate towards these individuals. If you can train the mule to allow people to ride him, you will see that they develop the most special bond with the people who are in these programs.

- **Baby sitter:** A mule makes for a wonderful babysitter as they love children. Unless you know of any kicking or biting history, a mule is good with children. They are very patient and are, hence, perfect to allow around kids. They are mostly used as therapy animals around children who are disabled. A female is most preferred for this because of the even temperament.

- **Working mule:** There are several jobs that your mule can carry out. The most common ones are riding, packing and recreational purposes. Many backpackers will have a mule accompany them on their adventures. Since they are able to carry heavy loads, they are ideal for these trips. The best thing about mules is that they can walk at human pace quite easily. They can carry farm material such as fencing, firewood, trash and other items. This transporting can be done with the help of panniers that are convenient in comparison to carts.

Bonding with your mule can be very fulfilling and a lot of fun. However, you will have to dedicate a lot of time and ensure that you are patient with your animal. They retain information for long periods of time and can become a great helping hand in your farm and pasture.

4. Perfect mule toys

While mules have often been labelled as stupid and dull, they are very good thinkers. They need a lot of mental stimulation in order to remain healthy. Now, it is easy for your mule to get bored. If you have a mule who is bored, he will pick up just about anything to play with.

In order to keep your mule happy, make sure that you have ample toys for him to play with. When they are able to keep themselves amused, they will give up habits like cribbing on the barn and fence. If you have a male mule, you have to be particularly concerned about the mental stimulation as they love to play hard. They can build up a lot of energy that is channelized in a negative manner when they do not have ways to release it.

Here are some toy ideas for your mule. They are inexpensive but will be loved by your pet:

- Empty cardboard boxes. You can even put treats inside these boxes and watch the mule have a great time.

- Milk jugs or water jugs made from plastic. Fill this with some colored water to amuse the mule.

- An old garden hose. Remove the metal ends to provide the animal with a safe toy.

- Cotton rope or cloth tied in knots. This is quite similar to the tug toy that you will provide a dog.

- Inner tube of the bicycle or a bicycle tire. Make sure any metal fill that is present is removed.

- Traffic cones that are brightly colored. These are the most popular toys as far as mules are concerned.

- Large sized balls that the mule can pick up with the mouth and kick around. A football is a great option.

When you have the right toys, you can make your mule very happy. A happy mule is also very obedient. Playing is one of the best forms of exercise for your mule. The more they are able to release energy, the calmer they are going to be in the long run.

Chapter 6: Transporting Mules

Whether you are bringing the mule home from the breeder's or if you have to transport the mule to another city or state because you have to move, you have to be very considerate as transportation can be very stressful for mules. You have to ensure that the mules are entirely comfortable during the journey to prevent any bad behavior or health issues when the trip comes to an end.

1.Transportation guidelines

Transporting livestock in general has several guidelines in the UK as well as the USA. Adhering to that is mandatory when it comes to private animals as well. These guidelines have been put into place to make sure that the welfare of the animal is also maintained when transporting. In case you are transporting the animal abroad, the vet will have to provide appropriate health certificates.

Loading the mule

For anyone who is transporting mules for the first time, loading the animal presents itself as the biggest challenge. Here are a few tips that can make it easier:

- Never rush the mule. When you try to push a mule who is hesitant into doing something, it usually spells trouble. No trick like luring him with treats or food will work. The best you can do is use a long lead that you can secure on a ring in the front of the trailer.

- Before you get the mule loaded in, tether him to the ring. You will need two people to get him into the trailer. One who will actually lead him into the trailer and another who can stop him from going back.

- Make sure that the ring is secured properly. You see, a mule can be extremely stubborn. So, if he decides not to enter and just back up, you will need the support of the lead.

- In some cases, the mule will enter the trailer only half way and freeze. This is when just two feet are in the trailer. This is frustrating as you only have two more feet to go. But the mule may not budge.

- In that case, you do not have to make it a big deal. Stay relaxed and move around calmly. Don't make too many noises like opening and closing doors as it will make the mule very suspicious and will prevent them from entering the trailer at all.

- Food must never be used to lure the mule. It is advisable to use treats when the mule enters. Only if you are not familiar with the mule can you use grass or grains to get him into the trailer.

In order to get the mule into a trailer, you need a lot of patience. Putting the trailer a place that the mule would feel comfortable is the first step towards getting him in.

Place a lot of bedding and keep the trailer clean. There should not be any flies or insects. Having a well-ventilated trailer is crucial if the day is warm.

Park your trailer in such a way that the mule cannot escape from the sides. The lower the height of the ramp, the easier it is on you. If this is your first attempt to transport your mule, make sure that you place him in the trailer and take small trips before you actually go on a long drive.

Tips for comfortable transport

- Use a basic trailer that is towed by a vehicle. Avoid journey durations beyound8 hours. If necessary, you can take breaks in between.

- If you are using a trailer that is borrowed, make sure that you check the floor, ramp, catches and lights for safety.

- Don't forget to check the capacity of towing of the trailer. That will help you plan the number of mules you can transport.

- The trailer must comply with all the legal requirements such as the cables, the brake, the tire, spare wheels and the registration plate.

- For journeys that are longer than 8 hours, there is a specially designed lorry. You can even choose a train journey or ferry if available.

- When travelling long distances, make sure that the mule has ample space, food, water and ventilation.

- The mule will use most of his energy trying to maintain his balance when traveling. So ensure that you drive as slowly as you can to reduce the stress caused to the animal. Pay attention to the acceleration, breaking and cornering.

- Make sure you choose a route that is smooth and can keep the journey continuous.

- The journey must be planned with a lot of care to make sure that you do not have any delays due to traffic. Any ventilation in the trailer occurs only when the vehicle keeps moving forward.

- Make plans to travel during the colder months of the year. Travelling in heat or scorching summers can be taxing for you and the mule.

- Make sure that that the bedding you have in the trailer will absorb the urine and feces completely. If it is not thick enough, you will have to clean it out frequently.

- Rubber matting is the best option when it comes to bedding to make it comfortable. You can add shavings to increase the absorption in the trailer.

- If you compromise on the bedding, the air quality in the trailer also reduces, making the journey very uncomfortable for the mule.

- The box must be cleaned thoroughly at the end of the journey to prepare it for the upcoming one.

- Never carry hay nets outside the trailer or the vehicle. They will absorb all the emissions of the vehicle and will become unhealthy to use with your mule.

- A fully charged mobile phone must be available at all times with the number of the contact person at the destination, emergency services in case of a breakdown, your vet and other relevant contacts.

- If it is possible to take an assistant with you who is familiar with your mules, do so.

- Any drinking water or bucket must be carried in the towing vehicle. Putting this in the trailer can lead to unwanted spilling.

- The passport of the mule must be carried in case you are stopped by authorities or if your mule needs medical attention.

- A spare leash and head collar is a must as you may have breakage and other issues.

- A fluorescent waist coat and torch is mandatory if you are travelling at night.

- Minor injuries are quite common when travelling. Carry a first aid kit that has all the contents mentioned in the following chapter.

- Your vehicle must have adequate fuel before you begin the journey.

Checking on your mule
There are a few things that you can do to make sure that your mule is not very stressed when travelling:

- The maximum stress is experienced by the mule when he is being loaded and unloaded. You can prevent this stress by planning these steps and carrying them out with helpers who have good experience.

- Carry damp hay for a long journey so that you can feed the mule when you are resting.

- The mule must be checked on every four hours without fail. You must offer water every 4 hours at least.

- Make sure you do not bandage the mule when travelling. This can lead to overheating. So, you will not need any rugs in most cases. It is a good idea to carry one, however.

- The mule should be fit to travel. You can check with your vet to ensure that your mule can travel long distances.

Veterinary assistance
Make sure you call a vet if you see any of these signs:

- Reduced appetite
- Nasal discharge or respiratory disorder
- Sickness
- Lameness

- If you are transporting a pregnant dam
- A young foal who is still sucking
- A young foal less than 1 week old.

Mule passports

In most parts of UK and Europe, travelling mules, donkeys and horses will require a passport. It is the job of the owner to make sure that their mule has a passport that is valid when making plans for long distance travel. Here are some tips to get a passport for your equine:

- Contact the Department of Environment Food and Rural Affairs or an equivalent authority in your country to check for authorities that issue passports to mules.

- Make sure that you fill out all the relevant paperwork after you have filed the application.

- You will have to provide details like the distinctive markings and a description of your mule.

- It is mandatory to have the mule micro-chipped. You can consult your vet for this.

- Your veterinary surgeon will have to provide a silhouette drawing of the mule for proper identification.

- You can even sign a statement that says that your mule cannot enter the human food chain.

- If you do not own the mule but are the keeper you will be logged as keeper in the passport.

- In case your keeper changes, make sure that your passport is updated accordingly.

Passports are mandatory and the failure to have one when travelling makes you liable for fine and also prosecution.

Important tips

There are a few points that you need to keep in mind when travelling with the mule:

- If your mule has any respiratory issues, it may become alleviated when travelling. Travelling leads to a lot of breathing issues in mules.

- The food and water intake of the mule may reduce significantly when you are travelling with a mule. This should be restored in a couple of days.

- Always have a map handy in case you have to change routes if the one that you have chosen is stressful to the mule.

- Any pre-existing health condition might increase due to the stress of travelling.

- Consult your vet about proper travelling precautions.

With these simple tips in mind, you are ready to travel safely with the mule. The primary goal is to make sure that you need to reduce stress and anxiety in the animal as much as possible.

Chapter 7: Mule Health

These stoic creatures are experts in covering up illnesses. So you have to be very attentive to notice the smallest deviation from the norm. When it comes to proper healthcare, it is the most important role that you will play as the mule owner.

In this chapter, you will come across the term zootonic quite often. This refers to diseases that can be transmitted from animals to humans.

We will talk about the symptoms of the diseases and understand the best ways to prevent them from occurring or from being transmitted.

1. Identifying a sick mule

The biggest challenge faced by mule owners is that they are stoic creatures. This means that identifying any sickness in your mule can be extremely difficult. They will show almost no signs of illness in the initial stages of contracting a disease.

There are three signs that you must watch out for:

- Sudden loss in appetite
- Depression
- Dullness

The last two are quite hard to understand because mules are, by nature, very docile and reserved creatures. You may often mistake depression for general behavior. This is why you need to make sure that you interact with your mule regularly. Even the slightest deviation from normal behavior indicates that you need to meet a vet immediately.

2. Common illnesses in mules

There are some diseases that are very common in horses and mules. You need to be very careful about identifying these conditions and helping the animal recover at the earliest. If you have a herd, especially, you need to be careful that the diseases do not spread from one animal to the other.

Tetanus or lockjaw

This condition occurs if the skin or the hoof is damaged. The microorganism causing tetanus lives in the intestines of the mule and can affect a mule who has been injured or has had a surgery. If your mule develops this condition, it is usually fatal.

Prevention:

- Provide an annual tetanus toxoid vaccine
- If the animal has had a surgery, provide a tetanus anti-toxin injection within 24 hours

Rabies

A mule with rabies becomes aggressive. There have been reports of accidents that have proved fatal to the human. This is a zootonic disease that often affects the brain of the animal. If your mule is bitten by a rabid skunk, dog, raccoon, fox or other animal, he can develop rabies. If a human is bitten by an affected mule, he can develop the condition. Treatment is a long process that lasts for several weeks. A rabid horse will also succumb to the condition.

Prevention:

- Get the animal an annual vaccine
- A brooding mare should be vaccinated just before breeding.

Encephalomyelitis

This condition is also called EEE or Easter Equine Encephalomyelitis, WEE or Western Equine Encephalomyelitis and Venezuelan Equine Encephalomyelitis or VEE.

This is another zootonic disease that affects the spinal cord and the brain of the affected animal. The condition is normally transmitted by mosquitoes from rodents and birds to equines. VEE is transmitted to human beings and not EEE or WEE. A horse affected by this condition usually succumbs or will have severely damaged nervous system.

Prevention:

- Annual vaccination for WEE and EEE
- Vaccination for VEE should be provided as per the recommendation of your vet.

West Nile Virus

This is another zootonic disease that affects the brain of the animal. It is transmitted from birds and rodents to the equines by mosquitos. Horses that are affected will die or will develop permanent damage to the nervous system.

Prevention:

- Annual vaccination

Equine influenza

The mule develops a high fever with these symptoms:
- Depression
- Cough
- Weakness

The appetite of the mule is affected and he may stop eating completely. Usually the mule will recover in about 3 days. However, symptoms will be seen for almost 6 months. In extreme cases, it is fatal to the mule.

Prevention:
- Have your mule vaccinated every 3-6 months

Rhino Virus Abortion

This is a strain of herpes virus that commonly affects equines. The symptoms include:
- Snotty nose
- Yellowish pus from the nose
- Dry Cough

If the broodmare is affected, it will damage or kill the fetus. If a young foal is affected, he may develop pneumonia and may even die.

Prevention:
- Every 6 months, have all mules that are under the age of 5 vaccinated.
- In the 5th, 7th and 9th month of pregnancy, all broodmares should be vaccinated.

Potomac horse virus
This is a condition that occurs when the animal ingests insects like mayflies, dragon flies, damselflies, stoneflies, snails or larvae of these insects. The common symptoms are:
- Lack of appetite
- Depression
- Dehydration
- Colic
- Diarrhea

If the horse is not vaccinated, he may succumb to the infection.

Prevention:
- Vaccinate the animal every year
- Do not let the animal drink from lakes or ponds
- The water troughs and buckets should be kept clean
- During seasons when there are several insects flying about, make sure you turn the lights off at night.
- Make sure that there are no dead insects in the food or water of the mule.

Equine Viral Arteritis
This disease is very common in mules that are breeding. If you are using methods like artificial insemination, the animal is still at the risk of developing this condition.

Prevention:
- Any stallion who is going to be bred should be checked 28 days before the breeding season.
- Only clean mares should be bred.
- In case of artificial insemination, the semen should be tested, especially when it has been imported.
- Vaccinate breeding stallions and mares annually

If the mare is vaccinated, the virus is still being shed from her body. That means they must be quarantined from the mares that are pregnant. A mare must never be vaccinated in the last 2 months of her gestation period. You must also avoid vaccinating a foal who is less than 6 months old.

Rotovirus
This is a disease that is very common in younger foals. If they are not treated in time, the foal may die.

Prevention:
- Pregnant mares should be vaccinated in the 10th month or 9th month of pregnancy.
- Visitors should be kept away from young foals
- Make sure that you wash you hands and keep your boots sterilized every time you handle the foal.

Distemper or strangles

A mule who is affected by this condition will exhibit these symptoms:
- A swollen throat
- Yellow snotty nose
- Cough
- Puss draining in the throat glands

This condition is not fatal in mules if they have been well maintained. The pasture that is used by these animals will remain infected for a long time, however.

Prevention:
- Annually vaccinate the mule.
- A nasal spray vaccination is a must for foals that are about 4 weeks old.
- Incoming horses or mules that look sick should be quarantined.
- When you are handling quarantined horses or mules and the resident mules, you need to make sure that you clean and disinfect your clothes and boots.

Botulism

If your mule has eaten any food that is moldy, rotten or spoilt, they can develop Botulism or food poisoning. It can also be caused when there are insects or other dead organic matter in the food. If your mule is affected, it may lead to death in 2-3 days.

Prevention:
- Make sure that all the food that you give your mule is free from any rotten spots of mold or insects.
- If you are feeding silage or hay bales to the mule, make sure that it is thoroughly checked.
- Broodmares must be vaccinated for botulism.
- Also get an opinion from your veterinarian about vaccinating foals.

Opossum Disease or Equine Protozoal Myeloencephalitis (EPM)

This is a disease that horses and mules develop when they consume opossum feces. It is a zootonic disease that can be fatal to horses and mules. When the mule is affected with this condition, the first symptoms are:
- Inability to coordinate between the limbs
- Loss of mobility in the hind limbs

Prevention:
- Keep the pasture clear of any opossums. You can place traps around the area.
- Make sure that the food containers have enough barriers around them.
- Never serve any food that has the slightest traces of feces or poop on it.

Clostridial Enerocolitis
If there is any change in diet or if your mule has been on antibiotics, this condition can occur. Even if he has been deprived of hay for a very long time, you will see the following symptoms:

- Swollen belly
- Colic pain
- Diarrhea
- Blood in stools

Prevention:
- Any change in feed should be gradual
- Oral probiotics must be administered to foals right after birth

Adenovirus
This is a disease that is normally seen in newborn foals. It is for the foals to receive the antivirus from the dam. If not it can be very serious. Initially, you will notice simple symptoms like:
- Labored breathing
- Mild cough

Prevention:
- Keeping the living conditions of young foals very clean
- Washing your hands and feet before handling foals

Pigeon fever
This condition is also known as dry land heavens and dry land strangles. The condition is called this because of the following symptoms:
- The midline has draining pus, abscesses and deep sores
- The swelling on the midline resembles the breast bone of a pigeon, leading to this name.

This disease is usually caused when the mule has any wound, broken skin or mucous membranes. When these wounds are circled by houseflies, the risk is higher.

The condition is most prevalent in the Western parts of the US.

Prevention:
- The mules that have been infected must be isolated
- The stall and the equipment must be disinfected fully
- Any biohazardous material or pus must be disposed.
- Make sure you wash your hands every time you handle the infected animal. Also disinfect the boots and garments you had on while handling them.

The diseases that we will discuss in the following section should be immediately reported to your vet. These are diseases that, as a law, need to be reported to a State or Federal Veterinarian.

Brucellosis
The first signs of this disease are fistula on the withers. While this disease is not spread by mules to humans, they are carried and transferred by sheep, pigs, deer, goats and other domestic cattle.

Prevention:
- If there is any cattle that is infected, you must keep it away from the mule
- The pastures must be fenced to prevent the entry of any wild pigs
- In the US, any cattle tested positive for this condition must be euthanized

Equine infectious anemia (EIA) or Swamp Fever
This is a condition that is mostly transmitted by horse flies, deer flies, saliva blood, body fluids, milk or unsanitary syringes and needles.

Prevention:
- An annual Coggins test must be conducted on horses
- If you are showing your mule, make sure that he is only taken to events where a negative Coggins Test report is mandatory
- All used syringes and needles must be disposed in a medical waste container.
- A horse or mule who tests positive for this condition may have to be euthanized as per the federal laws.

Vesicular stomatitis

This condition affects humans, livestock, mules and wild animals. It is usually transmitted by gnats and flies. You can also contract it if you come in contact with the equipment, feeding buckets or saliva of the animals that have been infected. This condition can be transmitted from mules to humans.

Prevention:
- Keep a check on insects
- Maintain individual feeders if possible
- Incoming or imported horses must be quarantined
- Horses that seem sick must be isolated
- When you handle these mules, make sure that you have latex gloves on as well as rubber boots. Disinfect them after you handle them and ensure that you change your clothes and thoroughly wash your hands before you handle healthy horses.

African horse sickness
This condition is prevalent in Africa. It is usually transmitted by mosquito bites. There are three forms of this sickness that display these range of symptoms:
- High fever
- Depression
- Cough
- Frothy discharge from the mouth and nostril
- Troubled breathing
- Swelling in the neck and head
- Pink eye
- Pain

Prevention:
- Consult the veterinarian about the potential of exposure in your area and also about necessary vaccinations.
- Any horse or mule that is being imported from Africa must be quarantined for at least 2 months and then tested.

Contagious Equine Meritis
This condition is acute and highly contagious. It is very prevalent in European countries. The stallions are usually carriers that will show no symptoms. The mares, on the other hand can show several symptoms including:
- Bleeding from the vulva
- Milky pus after about 14 days of breeding

- Failed impregnation
- Abortion

Prevention:
- Any mule who has been imported must be quarantined and checked
- If a mule has tested positive for CEM, you must not breed them until they are treated and declared "clean"
- Hygiene is of utmost importance when you are handling these mules.
- Disinfect instruments and use disposable gloves when you handle them
- If you suspect this condition in any of your horses, call the vet immediately.

Anthrax
This is a common condition with any cattle that grazes. If you come in contact with an infected animal or its products, you stand the risk of being infected too.

The condition is spread when the healthy animals come in contact with the nasal discharge of infected animals or consume contaminated food and grass.

The mules that develop this condition show the following symptoms:
- Swollen areas on the neck, belly and throat
- Chills
- Stupor
- Bleeding from the rectum
- Fast breathing
- Staggering
- Coma

It can be fatal to your horses and mules.

Prevention:
- Before the seasonal outbreaks of anthrax, have your mule vaccinated. You can consult your vet for this cycle.

Piroplasmosis
A mule will develop this condition when he is infected by a tick bite or by a reused needle. The infected animal will display these symptoms:
- Weakness
- Loss of appetite about one to two weeks after exposure
- Fever

- Anemia
- Yellowish coloration in the eyes and mouth
- Anemia
- Reddish urine

Prevention:
- All used needles and syringes should be disposed correctly
- Ticks should be controlled
- Remove and destroy all ticks from the infected animal
- If a horse or mule is tested positive for this condition, keep him quarantined at least 300 feet away from the healthy animals.
- Return the animal from quarantine only after he has been fully cleared of all the ticks on his body.
- Never use syringes that have been used before.

The above mentioned diseases will affect most equines. If you have a mixed stable, make sure that you have all the animals tested and vaccinated regularly.

Hypercalcemia
This condition is life threatening in mules. When the fat reserves are mobilized, they are sent to the liver where they are converted into energy yielding glucose. The issue with mules is that they are not great at stopping this mechanism and with time, the liver and kidney degenerate.

Decreased appetite is one of the only signs that the mule will display when he is hypercalcemic. There are some conditions that lead to this disease:

- Obesity: If the fat reserves are high, insulin is resisted. You need to monitor the diet of your mule and watch the weight very carefully.

- Age and gender: The older mules are at a greater risk of this condition and so are the mares.

- In case of late pregnancy or late lactation, this may occur.

- Diseases like Laminitis and Cushing's disease can lead to this condition.

- Other common factors are surgery, stress or any concurrent disease.

Prevention:

- Remove any condition that is causing stress.
- Exercise

Fluid therapy and dedicated care can reduce the symptoms caused by this condition in your mule. You must keep a regular check on the diet of your mule after he has been diagnosed with this condition.

Hoof and foot problems
The hooves of a mule are elastic, small, upright and tough. It is very common for mules to develop issues with respect to their hooves. But, with proper care, you can reduce the occurrence of this condition.

Genetically, mules have been used to living in arid conditions. So, in countries like Europe where the levels of moisture are high, it is common for the mule to develop foot abscesses, weakness in the walls of the hoof and also thrush. You will have to provide them with constant care to prevent these issues.

Laminitis is one of the most common foot problems in mules. It is common in mules who eat too much lush or frosty grass. You have to make sure that your mule gets high fibre and low sugar foods in order to prevent this condition.

Prevention:
- Provide dry bedding
- Ensure the stable is clean
- Fields should be well drained
- Trim the feet every two months to keep them in the best condition.

With these precautions, you can avoid problems that can even lead to lameness and decreased mobility in your pet.

3.Dealing with injuries
When your mules are free ranging on the ranch, there are chances that they will have injuries from time to time. You can treat the small bruises and wounds at home. However, when it comes to the larger and deeper wounds, it is best that you consult your vet.

Have a first aid kit ready
The first thing that you need to do is to keep a first aid kit handy on the pasture. You will need to have the following items in your mule first aid kit:

- Cotton wool
- Gauze swabs
- Animal lintex poultice material
- Equine cleansing or antiseptic solution
- Latex gloves
- Thermometer
- Vet's number
- Record of vaccinations

With these items in place, you will be able to treat the wounds of your animal quite easily. Make sure that you replace used items ASAP.

First steps to treating a wound
- Make sure you prevent further injury.

- Catch the mule and make sure you can calm him down. In case your mule is frightened you need to also stay aware of your own safety.

- Examine the wounds thoroughly. If you are examining the wound on the feet, be additionally cautious.

- In case of minor wounds, clean the wound up first with clean and cold water. This step helps control bleeding and also ensures that there is no swelling.

- The wound should be fully cleansed using a gauze pad. The antiseptic solution must be diluted as per the instructions on the pack.

- If there is any hair in the region around the wound, make sure that you cut it off carefully to prevent any contamination of the wound.

- Sprays and powders must never be used unless you have been advised to do so by your veterinary surgeon. These may push the dirt deeper into the wounds.

If you have any doubts about the wound being infected, make sure that you consult your vet. Keep an eye out for any unpleasant smell or discharge on the wound. After you remove the bandage, you have to keep examining the wound.

When the wounds are healing, they may cause some discomfort to your mule. This will lead to self-trauma in the form of itching, rubbing or biting the wounded area. You can ask your veterinary surgeon for assistance in this case.

In the case of serious injuries, you will have to cover it with gauze and apply pressure to prevent bleeding. If the blood seeps through the gauze that you apply, do not remove it. Instead, just add a second layer on it to keep the bleeding under control.

When should you call the vet
You must call your vet if you notice one or more of the following:

- Bleeding is excessive. If there is any wound on the lower legs, it will bleed profusely. Make sure you apply enough pressure on it with gauze before you call your vet.

- If the wound has punctured through the thick skin of the mule.

- If the wound is close to the joint.

- If the wound is below knee level or if it is severe.

- If the wound has been contaminated by dirt or any other material.

- If you notice inflammation, lumps, swelling or bruising without obvious signs of a wound, it can be a warning sign of other underlying health issues in the mule.

4.Dealing with broken bones
Just as in the case of the horse, a broken bone in a mule is also enough cause for concern. There are several reasons why your mule may have a broken bone:

- He might have a fall when walking or trotting

- It could be from a fight with another mule. One violent kick is enough to break a mule's bones

- Microfractures are caused due to wear and tear caused from the nature of work that the mules do on your pasture. This can heal if the mule is given time to recover.

- Chip fractures are common in mules and are usually due to orthopedic conditions. These chips are usually seen in the hock joint, fetlock and the knee of the mule.

Diagnosis of fractures
There are a few obvious signs of a fracture in a mule. This is what you need to look out for:
- You will actually hear the popping sound if you are around when the injury occurs. This is followed by swelling and pain in that region.

- Inability to walk

- Inability to apply any pressure on the area that is injured

- Wincing or moving away when you try to touch that area

Treating fractures
In most hairline and mircrofractures, rest is the only way to help the animal recover. This is successful in most cases.

However, with serious fractures, a screw is used to keep the bones in place. Specially designed steel equine screws can be used for the mule. Screws can be placed permanently or may be removed after the fracture has healed.

The removal of these screws depends entirely upon the degree to which the wound has healed and also the severity of the actual injury.

Plates can also be used for fractures in mules. These plates are usually removed for younger mules who will have to continue to work on farms and pastures. However, if the mule is old and can retire after the injury, then the plate is removed.

If the plate needs to be removed, it means that the mule will have to undergo another surgery. Of course, there is a lot of new technology in equine surgery such as bio-absorbable screws or titanium screws.

In most cases, a cast is placed if the only option is rest for the mule to recover. This includes a very light supportive bandage that is placed directly over the affected area.

Mule dental care

Any pain or discomfort in your mule's teeth can lead to negative behavior. Usually any change in the mule's behavior is due to bad equipment and the former. People use disciplining techniques when the real problem is associated with the health of the animal, particularly the condition of his teeth.

Now, teeth in equines push up against the jaw constantly. They will wear with grazing eventually. Therefore a hole or decay is not cause for concern as it will wear out in time. There are several other problems that may occur in the teeth or the mouth that require good treatment. It is best that you have the teeth of your mule checked regularly because, most often than not, it can lead to several other problems.

Signs of dental issues
- Sudden loss in body condition.
- Severe eating disorders. The mule will not be able to chew well or eat properly.
- You will notice undigested foods in the dung of the animal.
- There will be recurring digestive issues like colic pain.
- The mule will have foul breath.
- Constant head tossing shows that his teeth may be digging into the noseband.
- He will drool or foam at the mouth.
- You may notice discharge from one side of the nostril.

The discharge in the nostril is usually the result of an abscess or broken tooth that has become infected. This condition is quite serious and can lead to infections that will spread to the sinus cavity eventually. Your equine may have to undergo surgery in order to solve this issue to prevent any infections in the other parts of the body.

Usually, the incisors will never cause any issues. These are the nipper teeth in the front. The grinding teeth, the molars, are the ones that cause a lot of issues. They will wear and tear unevenly leading to several problems for the mule. They may form sharp edges that will cut the cheeks and also the tongue of the animal. This can be corrected by a process called floating where all the sharp edges are rasped. This process is not painful and mules will be comfortable with it.

The most common dental issues are:
- **Teeth shedding:** The caps or the deciduous teeth will remain on permanent teeth sometimes, leading to an uneven chewing surface.

This also leads to a lot of food getting trapped in the teeth leading to inflammation from the spiking jaw. For this, you will have to pull the caps out.

- **Missing teeth:** If the teeth do not have a surface that can grind opposite to them, they will pinch into the hole. This can be extremely painful for the animal.

- **Wolf teeth:** In most equines, the first premolars or the wolf teeth are missing. This is not the canine that is seen in the males. They will be seen in the upper jaw just in front of the grinding teeth. These are small formations but extremely sharp. The mule will be irritated by it. You can have these teeth removed by an equine dentist. If you are confident about handling the mule, you can also check this by inserting your finger in the space between the incisors and the molars. You will feel the presence of this tooth there.

- **Bolus:** If there is a lump of un-chewed food in the cheeks, it will cause inflammation and must be removed at the earliest.

- **Mouth abscesses:** This is seen if any teeth are lodged in the tongue or the mouth. You have to pull the seeds out and have the mouth hosed. This can lead to uneven surfaces that lead to cuts and wounds.

- **Old age:** When mules are older, they will need a lot of care. They are most prone to dental issues. The wear and tear in the tooth can lead to blindness and deafness as it leads to poor chewing. When equines are very old, they will wear out. This is when you will have to provide soft food and also vitamins to the animal. The good news, however, is that this wear and tear is a lot better in mules, leading to a longer lifespan.

Dental health of equines should never be ignored. If you are suspicious of any problem, you can consult your vet who should be able to suggest a qualified equine dentist.

5.Finding a good equine vet
Taking care of your mule means that you need to have him vaccinated regularly and even checked up thoroughly every year. For this, you have to find a specialist or an equine vet who can deal with specific health issues related to these animals.

A good equine vet will have these qualities:

- **Good communication:** An equine vet should be able to give you all the options available when it comes to getting your mule treated. A good vet should be able to tell you how a certain treatment works, what the advantages are and also the alternatives.

  They should be patient enough to explain every treatment process in steps and also describe the possible outcome and the support work that is needed after treatment.

  When you meet the vet for the first time, ask as many questions as you can. If they seem to have the same philosophy in terms of providing care for the mule, you can build a long lasting relationship.

- **Experience and education:** You need to know all the details such as the area that the vet specializes in, the college that they graduated from and the other details. You need to know how much experience the vet has and how many different kinds of cases they have handled.

  It is best to find a vet who is a part of the American Association of Equine Practitioners.

- **The general character:** The vet should have qualities like the desire to serve when you need them, integrity and of course intelligence. Now, there are other factors like how the vet talks, if they are too chatty or just the general personality. Choose one who will suit your level of comfort.

- **Ability to handle the mule:** This is the best mark of experience. Now, not all mules are easy to handle. If your vet loses his cool very easily, then you may not be able to have smooth procedures and check-ups. Some procedures are inherently stressful for a mule and a good vet will be able to find alternatives to do it thoroughly and easily.

- **Multi vet facility or solo practitioner:** This is an important decision to make. A solo practitioner is preferred by many as they will have the same vet seeing them each time. On the other hand, if you choose a multi vet facility, you will have access to specialists who have more experience.

  In a multi vet facility, you will also have access to better technology. The process is a lot more standardized and you will see that it is also a lot more sustainable.

- **Availability:** The biggest downside with solo practitioners is that their availability is limited. However, they can compensate for this with the best after hours management. In any case, you will have to discuss backup and emergency services with your vet.

  You must make availability a priority as in case of an emergency, that is what will come handy. You must also be reasonable with expectations. If the vet is handling a more severe case than yours, let them prioritize that case.

- **Check for additional facilities:** It is a good idea to check out all the facilities and surgical equipment available. The better the facilities, the better it is for you. Of course, the equipment is only as good as the handler. So a qualified vet should always be your choice over technology.

- **The specialization:** You must be aware of the specialization of your vet. For instance, you may have an equine only practice as well as a mixed animal practice. It is best that you choose an equine only practice as there is a lot to work on when it comes to mules and equines. However, if you are certain that your vet specializes in equines, working with other small species should not be a red flag in any case.

A vet is a very important part of your journey with your mule. In most cases, the extreme illnesses may not have a positive outcome and you may have to choose drastic measures like euthanizing the mule. That is when you will need complete support from your vet. In a sense, a confident and sensitive vet will empower you.

When choosing your vet, you need to keep proximity in mind. You should be able to rush your mule to the vet in an emergency. Even the best equine vet who is too far away is of no use. You can find a qualified Equine vet with the Get-A-DMV feature that is available on the official American Association of Equine Practitioners, www.aaep.org.

6.Preventing common illnesses
With most of the common illnesses that your mule may contract, the end result is always quite drastic and will claim the life of your mule if not treated ASAP.

Now, there are a few measures that you can take to control these common issues with your beloved pet:

- **Quarantine all incoming mules**: This applies to horses as well. It is necessary to keep the new equine in a separate stable for a few days to observe for the manifestation of any illnesses. If you suspect that your new mule has the slightest illness, consult your vet. Most often, the new mule will look absolutely fine in health when he comes to you. But he may be a carrier. Quarantining will give the disease time to manifest.

- **Keep the stable clean**: Make sure that you give your mule a clean environment to stay in. The stable and all the equipment should be cleaned on a regular basis. If you are handling a quarantined mule, make sure you wear gloves and rubber shoes that are sanitized. You may also want to change the clothes before handling your resident mules.

- **Provide clean food:** If there are any traces of dust, feces or dead insects in some food stuff, you must never feed it to your mule. The food containers must be protected from rodents and other pests who may transmit diseases through body fluids and their excreta.

- **Keep the pasture free from predators:** Most often, diseases are caused by predators who may leave droppings on grass, bite a mule or horse or even contaminate the food. You can speak to the forest authorities in your area to learn about the common predators in your area. Use appropriate fencing depending upon the type of predator you need to keep at bay.

- **Vaccinate the mules regularly:** Most of the fatal and zootonic conditions can be prevented with the appropriate vaccination. Here is a list of the important vaccinations along with their cost annually:

    - Tetanus- $2- $20/ £1- £10
    - EEE- $2- $20/ £1- £10
    - WEE- $2- $20/ £1- £10
    - VEE- $2- $20/ £1- £10
    - Rabies- $10- $20/ £5- £10
    - West Nile Virus- $35- $45/ £15- £20
    - Flu- $5- $50/ £2- £25
    - Rhino- $15- $25/ £8- £15
    - Botulism- $20- $50/ £10- £25
    - Potomac Horse Fever- $25- $40/ £10- £20
    - Strangles-$20- $50/ £10- £25

According to the American Association of Equine Practitioners, you have to vaccinate all the horses and mules at your stable for the above illnesses that are most common in them.

7. Getting insurance for your mule

Treatments for several health issues can be expensive starting from as high as $2000 or £1500. So it is best that you choose some form of insurance to take care of them unless you have enough contingency funds in place. Now, most insurance companies that offer pet insurance will have equine insurance that you can claim for medical expenses of your pet.

Here are some tips to choose the best insurance for your mule:

- Choose what you want to insure. Some mule owners will want to have a comprehensive policy while others may choose only specific requirements. The premium that you pay will depend upon what you want the insurance to cover.

- Check the age limit for insuring the mule. Some policies will require you to insure your pet before it reaches a certain age and will only cover injuries and medical expenses after the mule reaches a certain age. The insurance may not be valid for senior mules in some cases.

- Vet fees are the most important criteria when it comes to insuring your mule. However, you will have to look at other options like the treatments and procedures that are covered by the policy. For instance, in some cases you may have limits upon the number of times you can claim insurance for procedures like MRI scans. It is very important to choose the insurance based on the conditions, your budget and the things you can claim for.

- Check for insurance policies that cover for third party liability. In case any damage or injury is caused by your pet to people, property or other domestic animals, this will offer complete protection if you are found to be legally responsible.

- You must make sure that the insurance covers any requirement irrespective of whether the mule is being handled by you, your family and friends or a keeper.

- One important cover offered by equine insurance is permanent loss of use. This is necessary if your mule is a working animal on your farm. In case an illness or injury renders your mule incapable of carrying out certain activities on your farm, insurance can be claimed. There is usually an age limit for this claim that is between the age of 2 and 17 years.

- The insurance policy must cover standards like theft, straying and death. In these cases you can claim the market value unless the sum insured is of lower market value.

- You can opt for a personal accident benefit that will not only cover a rider but also family members, friends and keepers as a standard.

- The tack cover and saddle cover are a good idea to help you incase of any theft.

- If your mule draws a vehicle or a trailer, you can have that insured as well.

If you have more than one mule, you will also get discounts on the remaining herd. If you have several mules in one stable, it is a good idea to have them all insured under the same provider.

8. What is equine euthanasia?

As your mule gets older, you may have to deal with the terrible decision of euthanizing the animal. In several cases, physical issues lead to severe mental trauma that can even make your mule a threat to you and your family.

In most cases, emotions will creep in and you will begin to second guess this decision. However, it is best that you take the advice of the vet if you are dealing with serious issues with respect to your animal.

Now, there are several signs that will tell you that it is time to let go. Some will be obvious and the others will be a lot more subtle.

When to let go

If you see these signs in your equine friend, you must consider euthanasia as an alternative:

- A fracture in the long bone that is meant to bear weight. In most cases, even if the owner has access to funds and medical care euthanasia is an option if an adult mule has a broken leg.

- If the tissue in this long bone is broken due to a ruptured ligament, the damage is permanent.

- If the mule is in a lot of pain, he will exhibit behaviors like self-thrashing, mental disorders and even a loss in equilibrium. These side effects due to pain are not treatable.

- Any external evidence of trauma or shock in the form of gray blue, white or red colored gums, increased heart rate at rest, extremities that are ice cold, mental depression etc.

- Exposure of abdominal contents due to the improper healing of a surgery site or rupture of a body wall.

- A chronic condition such as difficulty in or excessive eating, urination, drinking and defecation that is not treatable even after repeated medical intervention.

- Any condition that leaves your mule unable to move, stand or even defend himself.

- Any condition that makes a mule aloof and disinterested in his companion. This is a sign of caution as companionship is as important as food to mules.

Methods of euthanasia

There are several painless methods that can help put your mule to rest without causing too much suffering.

Lethal injection

Advantages:

- This is the most humane and quiet method when done correctly.

Disadvantages:

- There are very few barbiturates that will shut the brain down before the rest of the body. Others may lead to suffocation or paralysis.

- Not all vets can provide barbiturates that are licensed.

- If the person injecting the horse does not do it correctly, it will have a very violent reaction.

- Sometimes, the drug may not work on the mule.

- If a house pet consumes any tissue or blood from the body of the animal euthanized with an injection, it can lead to them slipping into a coma.

Gunshot

Advantages:
- This is the most instantaneous and reliable method of euthanizing the animal.

- There is no real danger if other animals come in contact with the body of the deceased mule.

Disadvantages:
- There is a lot of social and emotional stigma attached to it.

- If the person euthanizing the mule is not skilled, it can be unsafe and also extremely inhumane.

Putting a pet mule to sleep can be one of the most challenging decisions you will ever take as a pet owner. However, in some cases it is the most humane thing to do in order to ensure that you do not cause further damage to the mule. You need to make sure that the body of the pet mule that is euthanized is buried or cremated properly for safety reasons.

Conclusion

Thank you for choosing this book. This book is the result of extensive research among existing equine owners to make sure that you get the most useful and practical information when it comes to handling your mule.

It is important for every mule owner to consider the risk involved in bringing a mule home.

These creatures are extremely powerful and need a competent handler. If you are not experienced, make sure that you gain some information about rearing mules before actually investing in one.

Once you are confident about handling mules, this book can be a great guide to ensure that you have a wonderful journey with your mule. It takes a lot of involvement to raise a happy and healthy mule.

But, if you succeed, you will have a fun and fuzzy companion for life.

References

Keeping yourself updated with all the information that you need about your mule is the key to keeping them in good health. There are several online sources that will help you stay updated with information related to proper care for mules. Some of them are:

www.ruralheritage.com

www.luckythreeranch.com

www.albertadonkeyandmule.com

www.fao.org

www.a-z-animals.com

www.grit.com

www.muleranch.com

www.horseandhound.co.uk

www.cowboyshowcase.com

www.spalding-labs.com

www.thebrooke.org

www.motherearthnews.com

www.muleteers.com

www.royaltine.com

www.forum.horsetopia.com

www.modernfarmer.com

www.hobbyfarms.com

www.omafra.gov.on.ca

www.americanmuleassociation.org

www.tractorsupply.com

www.predatorfriendly.org

www.jandohner.com

www.equinenow.com

www.nasma.us

www.longearsmall.com

www.thespruce.com

www.thebritishmulesociety.blogspot.com

www.oregonpioneers.com

www.paintedqhfarm.weebly.com

Copyright and Trademarks: This publication is Copyrighted 2017 by IMB Publishing. All products, publications, software and services mentioned and recommended in this publication are protected by trademarks. In such instance, all trademarks & copyright belong to the respective owners. All rights reserved. No part of this book may be reproduced or transferred in any form or by any means, graphic, electronic, or mechanical, including photocopying, recording, taping, or by any information storage retrieval system, without the written permission of the authors. Pictures used in this book are either royalty free pictures bought from stock-photo websites or have the source mentioned underneath the picture.

Disclaimer and Legal Notice: This product is not legal or medical advice and should not be interpreted in that manner. You need to do your own due-diligence to determine if the content of this product is right for you. The author and the affiliates of this product are not liable for any damages or losses associated with the content in this product. While every attempt has been made to verify the information shared in this publication, neither the author nor the affiliates assume any responsibility for errors, omissions or contrary interpretation of the subject matter herein. Any perceived slights to any specific person(s) or organization(s) are purely unintentional. We have no control over the nature, content and availability of the web sites listed in this book. The inclusion of any web site links does not necessarily imply a recommendation or endorse the views expressed within them. IMB Publishing takes no responsibility for, and will not be liable for, the websites being temporarily unavailable or being removed from the Internet. The accuracy and completeness of information provided herein and opinions stated herein are not guaranteed or warranted to produce any particular results, and the advice and strategies, contained herein may not be suitable for every individual. The author shall not be liable for any loss incurred as a consequence of the use and application, directly or indirectly, of any information presented in this work. This publication is designed to provide information in regards to the subject matter covered. The information included in this book has been compiled to give an overview of the subject s and detail some of the symptoms, treatments etc. that are available to people with this condition. It is not intended to give medical advice. For a firm diagnosis of your condition, and for a treatment plan suitable for you, you should consult your doctor or consultant. The writer of this book and the publisher are not responsible for any damages or negative consequences following any of the treatments or methods highlighted in this book. Website links are for informational purposes and should not be seen as a personal endorsement; the same applies to the products detailed in this book. The reader should also be aware that although the web links included were correct at the time of writing, they may become out of date in the future.